From Your Friends At **The MAILBOX®**

MAY

S0-ABA-996

A MONTH OF REPRODUCIBLES AT YOUR FINGERTIPS!

Grades 4–5

Senior Editor:
Thad H. McLaurin

Writers:
Rusty Fischer, Peggy W. Hambright,
Elizabeth H. Lindsay, Thad H. McLaurin,
Cindy Mondello, Patricia Twohey

Art Coordinator:
Clevell Harris

Artists:
Cathy Spangler Bruce, Pam Crane,
Nick Greenwood, Clevell Harris,
Mary Lester, Rob Mayworth,
Kimberly Richard

Cover Artist:
Jennifer Tipton Bennett

www.themailbox.com

©1998 by THE EDUCATION CENTER, INC.
All rights reserved.

ISBN# 1-56234-220-7

Manufactured in the United States

10 9 8 7 6 5 4 3 2

Table Of Contents

Geography Bee Or Bust!

May Free Time

MONDAY	TUESDAY	WEDNESDAY	THURSDAY	FRIDAY
Look around your classroom. Count the number of brunettes, blondes, and redheads you see. Make a bar graph to show your findings. 	The Tuesday of the first full week in May is National Teacher Day. In honor of this occasion, make your teacher a special card. FOR A VERY SPECIAL TEACHER...	How many synonyms can you find for the word *small?* Can you find and list at least ten? **SMALL**	Seventh-grader Benny Benson designed Alaska's flag, which was adopted on May 2, 1927. Design a new flag for your state. 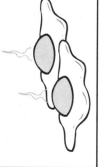 Texas	On May 7, 1986, Patrick Morrow became the first person to climb the highest mountain on each of the seven continents. Write a paragraph about something you'd like to be the first to accomplish. 
Mother's Day is observed the second Sunday in May. Write your mom or guardian a special poem thanking her for all she does for you. *Roses are red, Violets are blue . . .*	An *anagram* is a word that is made by changing the order of letters in another word. Make at least one anagram for each word below. CARE HEART OARS ARTS PART WORDS	May 12 is Eat What You Want Day. Create a menu for what you consider to be the perfect meal.	In 1989, Robert Commers set a world record by jumping rope 13,783 times in one hour. How many times can you jump rope in one minute?	May is National Egg Month. List the different ways you enjoy eating eggs.
In May of 1929 the first Academy Awards were presented. Nominate whom you think should receive the best actor and best actress awards this year and explain why.	Mt. St. Helens' volcano erupted in Washington state on May 18, 1980. Find out the names of at least two more volcanoes located in the United States.	May 22 is International Pickle Day. The word *pickle* can be used as a noun or a verb. Write two sentences: one sentence using pickle as a noun and another using pickle as a verb.	A *palindrome* is a word or phrase that reads the same backward or forward. List as many palindromes as you can. MOM POP RADAR	A banner day is a day when everything goes great! Write a brief paragraph about a banner day you've had. 
Onomatopoeia is a figure of speech that resembles the real sound to which it refers. Make a list of at least ten onomatopoeic words. 	The first color movie, *On With The Show,* debuted in May of 1929. Write a paragraph about the first movie you saw at a movie theater.	Add only one arithmetic sign (+, −, x, or ÷) to each equation below to make it true. 53491 = 625 48372 = 411 31402 = 6280 63903 = 2130	The Dionne quintuplets were born in Canada on May 28, 1934. Write a paragraph describing what it would be like to have four siblings your own age.  	A *phobia* is the fear of something. Use a dictionary to find the meaning of the following phobias: Acrophobia Arachnophobia Claustrophobia

Note To The Teacher: Have each student staple a copy of this page in a file folder. Direct students to store their completed work inside their folders.

MAY
Events And Activities For The Family

Directions: Select at least one activity below to complete as a family by the end of May.
(Challenge: See if your family can complete all three activities.)

Ducklings In Distress

Firefighters rescued 14 ducklings on May 9, 1988, in Warren, Michigan. The trapped ducklings were saved when a heavy sewer grate was removed and a firefighter climbed down into the sewer to get them out. Visit the library and research to find the names of other animals' babies, such as the oyster (spat), the swan (cygnet), or the kangaroo (joey). Then try to stump your parents: Tell them the name of the offspring and have them identify the parent. Conclude the activity by reading aloud to your family the popular picture book *Make Way For Ducklings* by Robert McCloskey.

Building Bridges

The Golden Gate Bridge, which spans San Francisco Bay, opened on May 27, 1937. It took four years to build and cost just under $35 million. Since it opened, more than one billion cars have crossed it. Challenge your family to find out more about the Golden Gate Bridge; then build your own suspension bridge. Gather materials for the bridge construction, such as drinking straws, yarn, pins, staples, craft sticks, and construction paper. Assign each family member a different task—attaching the cables, building the roadway, and so on. Then hold a special celebration for the grand opening of your bridge.

Fizzy Science

On May 8, 1886, Coca-Cola® was sold for the first time. Coca-Cola® and other soft drinks are carbonated, which means that carbon dioxide has been added to the liquid. The *fizz* results when the carbon dioxide gas is released and bubbles. Create some fizzy family drinks of your own by stirring one teaspoon of baking soda into a glass of lemonade or fruit juice.

PERSONAL HISTORY AWARENESS MONTH

Personal History Awareness Month is held every year in May. The purpose of this special occasion is to teach individuals and families about the importance of compiling a personal history.

A Star Is Born!

Make each student a star with this nifty idea. Have each student bring in a shoebox and two empty paper-towel tubes. Provide each student with a supply of 4" x 10" strips of paper, scissors, tape, and glue. Then have him follow the steps below to create his own movie box.

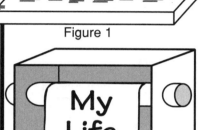
Figure 1

Steps:

1. Create a timeline on one strip of paper highlighting the important events in your life.
2. Paste the timeline to the top of the shoebox cover (see Figure 1).
3. Illustrate the title and each timeline event on a different strip of paper.
4. Arrange each strip vertically in chronological order; then tape the strips together.
5. Cut four holes in the shoebox; then insert the paper-towel tubes (see Figure 2).
6. Use tape to secure the top edge of the first movie strip to the top tube. Gently roll the paper-towel tube until the last illustrated strip is showing. Tape the bottom edge of the last strip to the bottom paper-towel tube (see Figure 2).
7. Place the cover on your shoebox.

Figure 2

School Day Memories

Help your students capture their school memories by completing this project. Give each student one 3" x 5" index card for each grade, kindergarten through the present grade. On the front of each card, have the student record the grade, the school, the teacher, and important memories from that class. Then have the student paste the cards in order onto a colored sheet of poster board. Next instruct the student to paste or tape one 3" x 2 1/2" black construction-paper rectangle on each end of each index card as shown to create shutters. Encourage each student to embellish her school by adding doors, shingles on the roof, etc. Display the completed schoolhouses for everyone to enjoy.

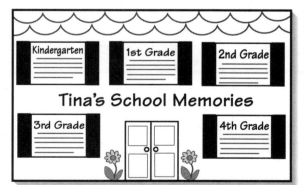

A Time Capsule Of My Life

Discuss with your students the purpose of a time capsule. Ask each student to bring in an empty, clean can with a removable lid. Have the student decorate his time capsule with illustrated scenes or photographs of important events in his life. Next have the student fill his can with items that he wants future generations to find. Encourage each student to share his completed capsule with the class, telling about the significance of each selected item. Have the class predict what students 100 years from now will think about their time capsules.

A Family Tree In The Forest Of Life

Families come in all shapes and sizes. Each family is special in its own way. Make your own family tree by following the directions below.

Directions: Cut out the tree pattern along the dotted line and paste it onto a piece of 12" x 18" colored paper. Print each family member's full name on one of the blocks below; then cut out each block. Paste each block in the appropriate space on the tree to show how that person fits into your family. If you have a large family, make more blocks if needed.

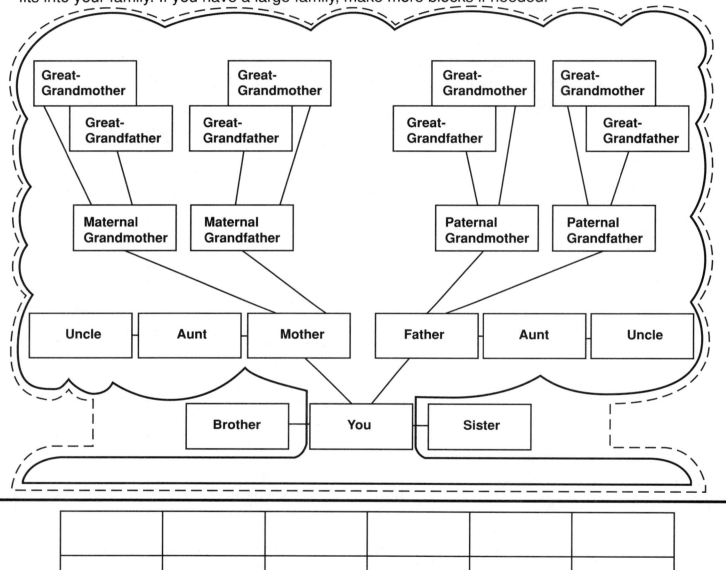

Bonus Box: Research to find out where each family member was born. Record the information in the appropriate box on the tree.

Note To The Teacher: Provide each student with a 12" x 18" sheet of colored construction paper, scissors, and glue. Display the completed family trees on a bulletin board titled "A Forest Of Families." Have students who come from fragmented families design their own special family trees on separate sheets of paper.

Name _____

Standing Tall

Like eye color and nose shape, your height is determined by the *genes* you inherit from your mother and father. Genes are tiny cells that act like a set of blueprints or directions for building your body. Find out how tall the members in your family stand, and complete the activity below.

Directions:
1. Choose four to six adult relatives in your family.
2. Write their names on the graph below.
3. Color in the bar graph to show each relative's height.
4. Next calculate an average height of the relatives listed below. Based on this average, make a prediction about your height as an adult.
   Predicted Height = _____
5. Show your prediction by coloring in your section of the graph.

FAMILY HEIGHT RECORD

7 Feet						
6¹/₂ Feet						
6 Feet						
5¹/₂ Feet						
5 Feet						
4¹/₂ Feet						

Relative 1	Relative 2	Relative 3	Relative 4	Relative 5	Relative 6	Your Predicted Adult Height

Note To The Teacher: Duplicate one copy of this page for each student. Send the page home at the beginning of the month. Specify a due date for students to complete and hand in their work.

Up Close And Personal

Have you ever wondered about your family's history? Well, now's the time to find out! Choose four older members of your family to interview. Read the questions below. Use a separate sheet to interview each relative. Take notes during each interview on the notepad at the right. After you have completed all the interviews, use the information to compile a short booklet about your family's history.

Name of relative you interviewed:

_____

1. In what year were you born?

2. Where were you born?

3. Where have you lived?

4. Describe the elementary school that you attended.

5. What types of sports or games did you play at school with your friends?

6. Did you have a pet? If so, what was it?

7. Describe your favorite memory of your childhood.

8. Describe a special family tradition.

9. Do you have a favorite family recipe? If so, what is it?

10. What would you like people to remember about our family?

11. What kind of work do you do?

12. Do you have any hobbies or interests? If so, what?

13. Do you have a special talent or skill? If so, what?

14. If you had one wish, what would it be?

©1998 The Education Center, Inc. • *May Monthly Reproducibles* • Grades 4–5 • TEC954

Note To The Teacher: Duplicate four copies of this page for each student. Send the pages home at the beginning of the month. Specify a e date for students to complete and hand in their work.

National Physical Fitness And Sports Month

Celebrated May 1–31, National Physical Fitness And Sports Month encourages individuals and organizations to promote fitness activities and programs.

Recipes For Fitness Fun

Mix a little exercise with a measure of fun, and you've got a recipe for a batch of physically fit students! Explain to students that being physically fit helps them meet the physical demands of daily life, resist diseases associated with inactivity, perform well in sports and other activities, and look and feel their best. Have the class list their favorite physical activities on the chalkboard, such as jumping rope, riding a bicycle, or playing basketball. Then distribute an enlarged copy of the recipe pattern on page 10 and the directions at right to each student. Have the student choose one activity listed and create a recipe for playing it like the example shown. Afterward take the class to the school gym or playground, and provide each student with the equipment listed on her recipe card. Then divide students into small groups and have group members test one another's recipes for accuracy.

Directions For Each Student:
1. Create a title for your recipe.
2. On the back, write a short introduction that describes the activity you will explain.
3. List all the equipment or materials needed to carry out the activity.
4. Describe each step of the activity. Add pictures or diagrams to help explain any steps that need clarifying.

Recipe For Fitness Fun From ___Scott___
(student's name)

___Hopscotch___
(name of game)

Equipment: large area of sidewalk; chalk; game marker for each player, such as a pebble, coin, or bottle cap

Directions:
1. Use chalk to draw 10 squares on the sidewalk. Make the squares large enough so players have room to hop in them without stepping on a line.
2. Number each square from 1 to 10.
3. Have each player gather a marker and place it near the first square.
4.
5.

Snapshots In Sports History

Sports have provided recreation for people throughout the world for centuries. Have the class brainstorm a list of their favorite sports, such as baseball, basketball, and hockey. Record their responses on the chalkboard. Then provide each student with three copies of the snapshot pattern on page 10, markers or crayons, scissors, glue, and a 12" x 18" sheet of colored construction paper. Assign each student a different sport to research. Direct the student to illustrate an interesting fact about his assigned sport's history and write an accompanying caption on each snapshot. Have each student cut out his snapshots and glue them onto the construction paper. Have students share their findings; then post the completed pages on a bulletin board or bind them in a booklet titled "Snapshots In Sports History."

Patterns

Use with "Recipes For Fitness Fun" on page 9.

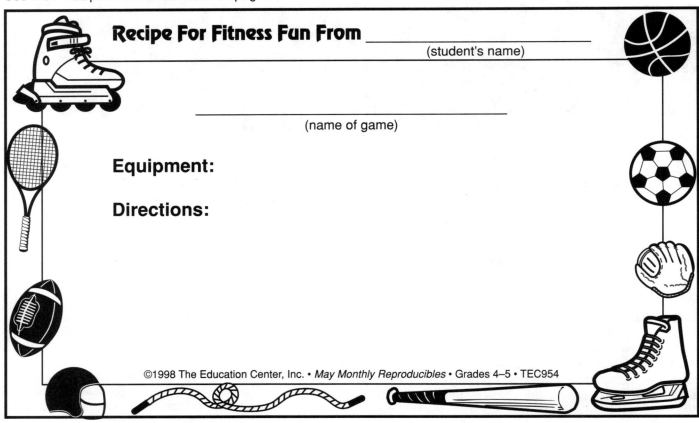

Recipe For Fitness Fun From _____
(student's name)

_____
(name of game)

Equipment:

Directions:

©1998 The Education Center, Inc. • *May Monthly Reproducibles* • Grades 4–5 • TEC954

Use with "Snapshots In Sports History" on page 9.

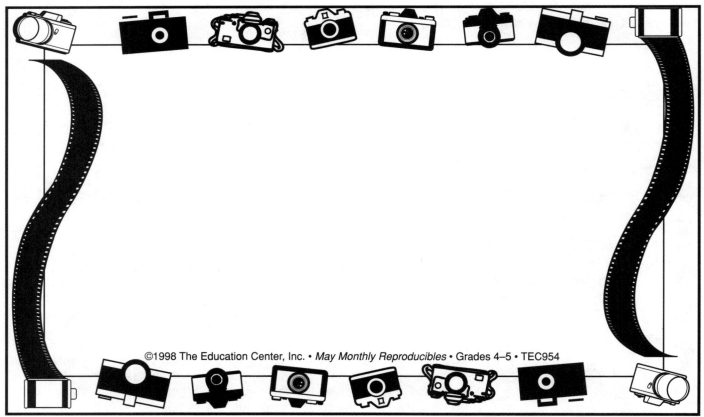

©1998 The Education Center, Inc. • *May Monthly Reproducibles* • Grades 4–5 • TEC954

National Physical Fitness And Sports Month: Food Guide Pyramid; critical thinking

Getting Your Daily Dose

Are you getting your daily dose of the right kinds of foods? Give your diet a checkup by keeping a one-day record of the foods you eat. Record the foods you eat for breakfast, for lunch, for dinner, and at snacktime on the chart below. Then, using the circled letters on the Food Guide Pyramid, write the letter or letters for each food's group. (See the example.) Use the back of this sheet if you need more space to write.

Example: milk (D)
fries (V) (FS)
hamburger (P)
bun (G)
lettuce (V)
tomato (F)
mayonnaise (FS)

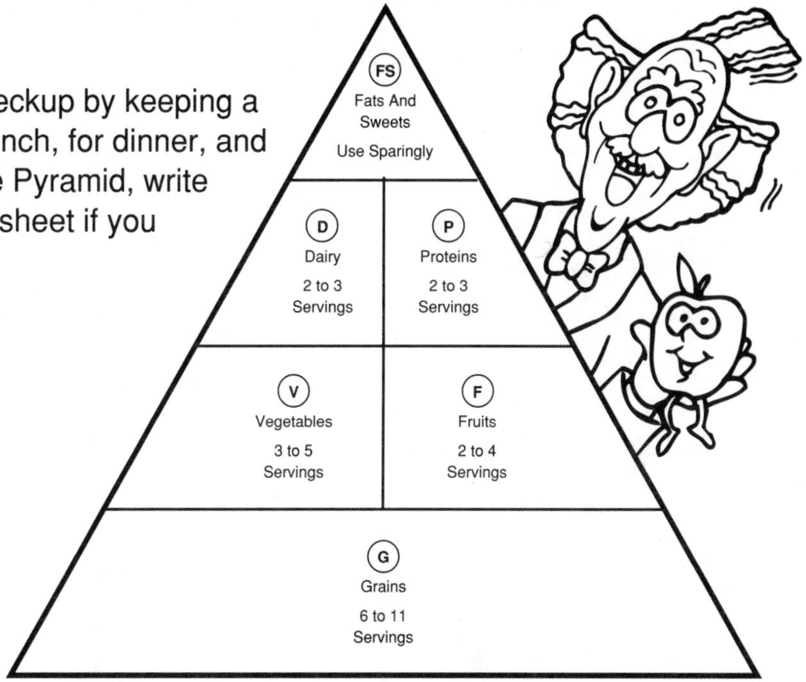

Food Guide Pyramid

(FS) Fats And Sweets — Use Sparingly

(D) Dairy 2 to 3 Servings
(P) Proteins 2 to 3 Servings

(V) Vegetables 3 to 5 Servings
(F) Fruits 2 to 4 Servings

(G) Grains 6 to 11 Servings

Breakfast	Lunch	Dinner	Snacks

Bonus Box: On the back of this sheet, list the total number of foods you have eaten for each food group. Is your diet "just what the doctor ordered"? Explain.

©1998 The Education Center, Inc. • *May Monthly Reproducibles* • Grades 4–5 • TEC954

11

National Physical Fitness And Sports Month: calculating pulse rates

Getting The Beat On Heart-Healthy Exercises

Your heart is a muscle that rhythmically pumps nutrients and oxygen-rich blood throughout the cells of your body by way of the blood vessels. *Aerobic* activities—such as walking, running, and bike riding—help to make the heart muscle strong.

Directions: Keep track of the kinds of aerobic exercises you participate in throughout one week. Fill in the information on the chart below, remembering to record a **resting pulse rate** *before* beginning each exercise and to record a **peak pulse rate** immediately *after* completing each exercise.

Example:

Time	Activity	Resting Pulse Rate	Peak Pulse Rate
30 minutes	skating	80	100

To Find To Your Pulse Rate:
First find your pulse by placing two fingers side by side on your Adam's apple. Then slide them into the groove on the side of your neck. Hold your fingers in place until you find a steady beat. Then count the number of beats you feel for six seconds. Multiply that number by ten to get a resting or peak pulse rate.

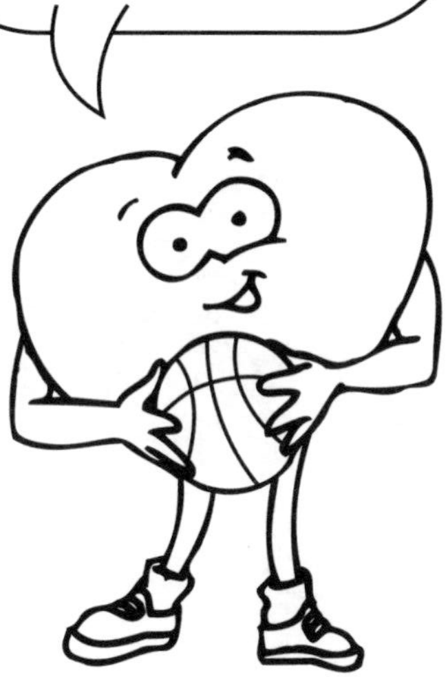

Did You Know?
Pulse is the push of blood through the blood vessels of the body. *Pulse rate* is the number of times the heart pumps each minute. Because the heart pumps faster during exercise, the pulse rate increases

Note To The Teacher: Use the directions above to help each student find his or her pulse before beginning the activity. Direct each student to use a clock, wristwatch, or stopwatch with a second hand to time each six-second interval.

Name _____

Problem-Solving Shape-Up

Regular exercise helps keep your body in tip-top shape. Give your brain a boost with this problem-solving workout!

Directions: Use one of the strategies listed below to help you solve each problem. Solve the problem on the back of this sheet. Then draw the strategy symbol in the box and write your answer in the blank.

Problem-Solving Strategies

Guess And Check—Sometimes several guesses must be tried before finding the correct solution.

Draw A Picture Or Diagram—Drawing a picture instead of just reading a problem may help you see it more clearly.

Identify A Pattern—Finding a pattern (a repeated arrangement of things) may help solve a problem.

Make A Graph Or Table—A table, chart, or graph helps organize and compare bits of information.

Make An Organized List—Listing information helps ensure that choices are not repeated or left out.

1. Twenty-five bicycles and tricycles are entered in a neighborhood road race. There are 62 wheels in all. How many of the entrants are bicycles, and how many are tricycles?

2. Gina jogs the same rectangular route every day. Starting at her house, she jogs 5 blocks north to the library. She continues jogging 7 blocks north to the museum, then 4 blocks east to the movie theater before jogging back home. How many blocks does she jog back home? How many blocks does she jog in all?

3. Weak Willy wants to lift weights. Use a triangular arrangement like the one shown to arrange the numbers 1–6 so that the sum along each side is 9 pounds.

4. Bob Billings loves bowling! The number of pins he knocks down always follows a pattern. Write a sentence to describe his latest pattern; then write the next three numbers in the pattern: 1, 3, 7, 13, 21, _____, _____, _____.

5. The Franklin High School football team wants to build a pyramid for their yearbook photograph. If the pyramid they build has 8 players on the bottom and 1 player at the top, how many players are on the team?

6. The product of the numbers on two players' jerseys is 91. The sum of the two numbers is 20. What are the two numbers?

7. Four members of the swim team swam the 50-meter freestyle in 60 seconds, 58 seconds, 65 seconds, and 72 seconds. Sally swam 65 seconds. Sam did not swim 58 seconds. If Sue swam 60 seconds, how many seconds did Sean swim? Sam?

8. The coach of the Archville Archery Team told four team members—Alexis, Brad, Connie, and Don—to work in pairs. List the different pairs that are possible.

Name _____

National Physical Fitness And Sports Month:
student activity calendar

Put Some Muscle Into Your Month!
MAY

Directions: Complete one activity each day. Lightly color the box after you complete each activity. Hand in the sheet at the end of the month.

Monday	Tuesday	Wednesday	Thursday	Friday
Do 10 jumping jacks. Then do 15 sit-ups.	Balance on your right foot. Grab your left ankle with your left hand, and put your right hand high in the air. Hold this position for 15 to 20 seconds. Repeat this with the opposite legs and hands.	Choose an activity such as jump roping or hopping. Count how many times you jump or hop before you take a rest. Repeat this, trying to jump or hop longer each time.	Play a game—such as kick ball, hopscotch, or tag—with your family or friends.	Choose an aerobic activity, such as bicycling or jogging. Do the activity for at least 15 minutes.
List three fitness goals. Then develop a plan to help you achieve these goals.	Keep a record of the snacks you eat for one week. Then make a list of healthful foods to eat in place of the not-so-healthful ones.	Make a circle using a four-foot piece of rope or yarn. Stand 10 to 15 feet from the circle and toss a ball toward it. Practice throwing the ball into the circle.	Lie on your back with your hands at your sides and your eyes closed for one minute. Breathe in and out slowly as you imagine a relaxing scene, such as a beach or mountain.	Line up ten empty soda cans or plastic bottles in a triangular pattern. Stand ten feet away from the "pins" and roll a small ball. Repeat this, trying to increase the number of pins you knock over each time.
Balance a book on your head. Walk around a room in your house. See how long you can balance the book before it falls.	Create a new dance. Teach the dance to a member of your family or a friend.	Choose an activity from a previous box. Do the activity again.	Place a ball on the ground. Make a figure eight by rolling it around your feet with your fingertips. Repeat this five times.	Role-play five actions that describe your favorite sport. Share the actions with a friend to see if he or she can guess the sport you are role-playing.
Hold a ball between your knees. Choose a goal line; then jump like a kangaroo until you get to the line and back again.	Take a 20-minute walk with a partner.	Practice dribbling a basketball five different ways, such as hitting it to the floor with your fist or hitting it to the floor with your hand and clapping before you catch it.	Create a relay race that includes five different movements, such as hopping, skipping, and crab walking.	Create five movements that portray objects such as clouds, waves, or falling leaves.
Exercise to your favorite song. Alternate walking, jogging, and resting until the song ends.	Do five sit-ups, five push-ups, and five trunk twists.	Play catch with a partner. Name an action for your partner to do before catching the ball, such as clapping, hopping on one foot, or turning around.	Crush a sheet of paper into a ball. Place a wastebasket five feet in front of you. Practice your freethrowing skills using the paper and the wastebasket.	Practice a skill—such as catching, throwing, or kicking a ball—for 15 minutes.

©1998 The Education Center, Inc. • *May Monthly Reproducibles* • Grades 4–5 • TEC954

Note To The Teacher: Use this calendar at the beginning of National Physical Fitness And Sports Month. Label each day's date in the corner of its box; then duplicate a class set. Give each student one copy of the programmed calendar and one file folder. Have each student complete one activity each day. Instruct each student to keep his calendar and completed work inside the folder. Collect the folders on the last day of the month.

NATIONAL HAMBURGER MONTH

Each May, National Hamburger Month is sponsored by White Castle, the original fast-food hamburger chain, to honor one of America's favorite foods.

Literal Lists

Is a hamburger really made out of ham? Of course not! But wouldn't it be funny if every word spoken were taken literally? Have your students brainstorm a list of words that if taken literally would have an entirely different meaning, such as *butterfly, hot dog,* and *chocolate shake.* After the list has been compiled, give each student one sheet of drawing paper and crayons or markers. Then instruct the student to select one word and illustrate its literal meaning. Post the completed illustrations around the room or on a bulletin board.

I've flipped for National Hamburger Month!

Have It Your Way!

Make your students' taste buds tingle with this mouthwatering activity! Provide each student with a copy of the pattern on page 16. Tell the student that he has been selected as the menu designer for his town's newest hamburger joint. Have him choose a theme for his restaurant, such as space, rock and roll, or fantasy. Then have him use words related to the theme to describe the items on his menu. For example, if he chose the theme of space, some featured items might be moon burgers or shuttle shakes. Have him complete the menu, then add illustrations that are appropriate to his theme. Display the completed menus around the room.

Patty-Melt Poetry

Mmm-mmm good! Have each student create his own story poem using hamburger-related words. Provide each student with a copy of page 17. Instruct the student to choose a hamburger-related word from the list, then write it vertically along the left-hand side of the bottom half of the sheet. Then instruct him to use each letter to begin a new line in a story poem about hamburgers. See the example below.

My Hamburger Poem
Barbecues are great
Under a huge
Red umbrella, while Dad
Grills a big, fat burger for
Everybody, even my ugly uncle,
Ralph!!
by Rusty

15

Pattern

Use with "Have It Your Way!" on page 15.

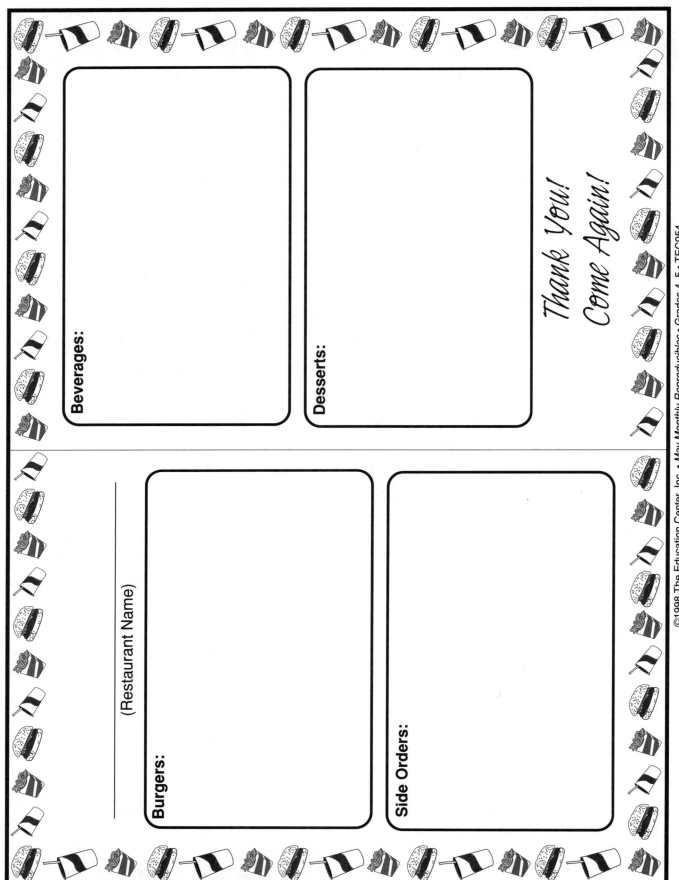

Beverages:

Desserts:

Thank You! Come Again!

(Restaurant Name)

Burgers:

Side Orders:

Hamburger-Related Words

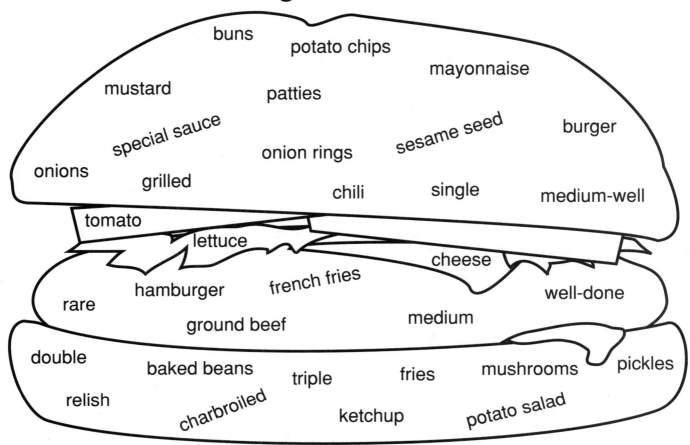

buns
potato chips
mayonnaise
mustard
patties
special sauce
onion rings
sesame seed
burger
onions
grilled
chili
single
medium-well
tomato
lettuce
cheese
hamburger
french fries
well-done
rare
ground beef
medium
double
baked beans
triple
fries
mushrooms
pickles
relish
charbroiled
ketchup
potato salad

My Hamburger Poem

Note To The Teacher: Use with "Patty-Melt Poetry" on page 15.

Name _____

Burger Barn Bonanza

Bif and Bart love to eat at the Burger Barn on a regular basis! The only problem is they never know how much they can buy with the money in their pockets. Help them solve each problem below. Read each problem, guess the answer, and then check it. Continue guessing and checking until you make a correct guess. Remember, there may be more than one correct answer for each problem.

Welcome To The Burger Barn!

(Prices Include Tax)

Burgers
Single	$1.00
Double	$2.00
Triple	$3.00

French Fries
Small	$.50
Medium	$1.00
Large	$1.50

Beverages
Small	$.65
Medium	$.85
Large	$1.15

Value Meals
Macho Meal	$3.50
Munchkin Meal	$1.75

Desserts
Cookie	$.50
Brownie	$1.00
Ice-Cream Cone	$1.50

Directions: Answer the following questions using the information on the Burger Barn's menu board. Use the back of this sheet if you need more space.

1. If Bart spent $10.00 on five items for Bif's birthday meal, what did he buy?

   _____

2. If Bif spent $5.85 at the Burger Barn, what did he buy?

   _____

3. If Bart spent less than $2.00 at the restaurant one day after school, what did he buy?

   _____

4. If Bif bought a beverage and a dessert for $1.35, which items did he buy?

   _____

5. If Bart bought three beverages and two food items for less than $6.00, what did he buy? _____

   _____

6. If Bif spent $8.75 on six items for Bart's birthday, what did he buy? _____

   _____

Cinco De Mayo

Cinco de Mayo—the Spanish translation for May 5—is a day of celebration for Mexicans. The holiday recognizes the anniversary of the date (May 5, 1862) the Mexican army defeated French forces at the city of Puebla. Today people of Mexican descent everywhere celebrate this victory with bands, fireworks, and reenactments of the battle.

South-Of-The-Border Map Game

Play this map game to become better acquainted with the physical geography of Mexico. Divide students into four or five teams, and provide each team with an up-to-date map of Mexico. Begin the game by naming a location in Mexico. One student on each team searches the map and tries to find the location without help from his teammates. The first team to find the location earns two points; other teams that find the site are awarded a point each. If after a minute no player has found the site, say, "Switch." The map is passed to a teammate who then tries. If after three switches no one has found the location, give clues. The game moves quickly, so be sure to have the next location ready! As an extension, provide only the location's latitude and longitude, and have students give the location's name.

Mexican Jumping Beans

Create a free-time center to which students will flock to learn Spanish words. Using a red, permanent, fine-tipped marker, label 55 lima beans with the Spanish words listed below. Using a black marker, label 55 more beans with their English translations. Store the beans in a plastic container (with a lid) decorated to resemble a piece of pottery. Make a self-checking key on an index card. Laminate the key; then store the key inside the container along with the beans. Invite students to spill the beans, match the words, and check their matches with the key. Olé for language!

green *verde*	four *cuatro*	book *libro*	recess *intermisiór*	spoon *cuchara*
blue *azul*	five *cinco*	pencil *lápiz*	desk *bufete*	fruit *fruta*
red *rojo*	six *seis*	test *examen*	blackboard *pizarra*	cookies *galletas*
yellow *amarillo*	seven *siete*	please *por favor*	library *biblioteca*	hamburger *hamburguesa*
orange *anaranjado*	eight *ocho*	number *número*	lunch *almuerzo*	bread *pan*
white *blanco*	nine *nueve*	school *escuela*	beverage *bebida*	potatoes *patatas*
black *negro*	ten *diez*	door *puerta*	cake *bizcocho*	French fries *patatas frita*
brown *moreno*	girl *muchacha*	window *ventana*	sandwich *bocadillo*	chicken *pollo*
one *uno*	boy *muchacho*	listen *escuchar*	candy *caramelo*	desserts *postres*
two *dos*	house *casa*	Spanish *español*	dinner *cena*	soup *sopa*
three *tres*	teacher *instructor*	English *inglés*	food *comida*	vegetables *vegetales*

Traveling Through Mexico

After celebrating Cinco de Mayo, Carlos, Luis, Maria, and Rosita visited different parts of Mexico. One went to a bullfight in Mexico City, one to a national park near Monterrey, one to the Yucatán Peninsula, and one to Lake Chapala, Mexico's largest lake. Find out where each student went.

Directions: Read the clues for the puzzle. Then go through the clues again one at a time. Use the clues to fill in each box on the chart with YES or NO. Fill in the blanks.

Clues:
1. No girl went to Mexico City.
2. One of the girls spent much of her time in the Yucatán Peninsula.
3. Luis has never been interested in parks.
4. Carlos did not visit the national capital.
5. Maria enjoyed watching boats on the lake.

	Mexico City (bullfight)	Monterrey (national park)	Yucatán Peninsula	Lake Chapala
Carlos				
Luis				
Maria				
Rosita				

Carlos visited_____.   Luis visited _____.

Maria visited _____.   Rosita visited _____.

What did each tourist carry on his or her trip? Use the following clues to solve this puzzle.

Clues:
1. A girl carried a tape recorder.
2. The boy with a backpack brought along books to read.
3. Maria didn't bring any postcards.
4. The person who visited the Yucatán Peninsula didn't have a camera.
5. The student who visited the national park took along a video camera.

	Video Camera	Postcards	Backpack	Tape Recorder
Carlos				
Luis				
Maria				
Rosita				

Carlos took _____.   Luis took _____.

Maria took _____.   Rosita took_____.

Note To The Teacher: Work through Clue #1 in the first puzzle together. For example, ask, "If no girl went to Mexico City, where can we write NO? Write NO in the Mexico City column beside Maria and Rosita's names." Continue working the sheet together if desired.

Sombrero Glyphs

In Mexico Cinco de Mayo means it's fiesta (or party) time! Young and old alike listen to bands, fill piñatas with candy and small toys, and enjoy fireworks. Share how you celebrate a favorite holiday by making a *glyph* (a symbol whose features are decorated to give specific information) from a sombrero pattern.

Materials: 1 sombrero pattern, scissors, glue, crayons or markers, colorful scraps of construction paper or fabric

Directions: Cut out the sombrero pattern. Decorate the sombrero according to the directions in the key below.

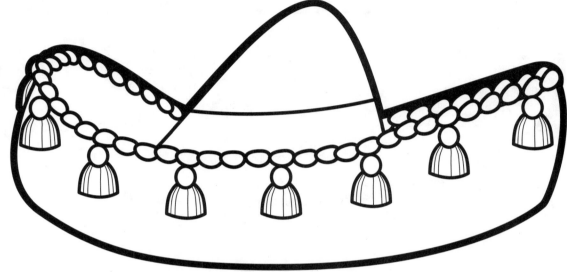

Sombrero Glyph Key

1. Color of hat = favorite holiday
    - brown = Halloween
    - orange = Thanksgiving
    - red = Christmas
    - pink = Valentine's Day
    - green = Easter
    - blue = Other

2. Color of edging around brim of the hat = the time you go to bed or get up on this holiday
    - gold = stay up late
    - silver = get up early
    - black = both
    - purple = neither

3. Color of tassels on hat = the most important part of this holiday to you
    - gold = the meaning
    - silver = what I eat
    - black = the decorations and fun

4. Decorations on hat (any color) = the kind of weather you prefer for this holiday
    - crown = snowy
    - square = rainy
    - flower = windy
    - triangle = cloudy
    - sunburst = sunny

5. Number of decorations on hat = how much you look forward to this holiday
    - two = a lot
    - three = more than a lot
    - four = more than I can say

6. Band around top of hat = favorite food to eat during this holiday
    - wavy = meat, poultry, or fish
    - diagonal = vegetables
    - circular = fruits
    - diamond shaped = breads
    - zigzag = desserts/candy

Note To The Teacher: Provide each student with one copy of this page, the materials listed, and an enlarged copy of the sombrero pattern on page 22. Have the student decorate his hat pattern according to the key on this page. Display students' projects on a wall or bulletin board. Extend the activity by having groups of students graph the different attributes shown by the glyphs.

Pattern

Use with "Sombrero Glyphs" on page 21.

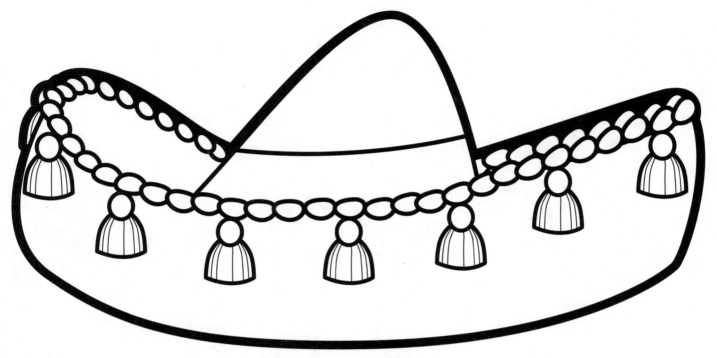

Name _____ Cinco de Mayo: math practice

Piñata Practice

A *piñata* is a decorated container filled with candies, fruit, or small toys that is hung from the ceiling and broken as part of a Mexican celebration. Blindfolded children try to break open the piñata by hitting it with a wooden stick. Where do you think this piñata will break?

To find out, solve the equations below. (Hint: Look for a solution that makes you think of the name of the holiday: Cinco de Mayo.) Have fun!

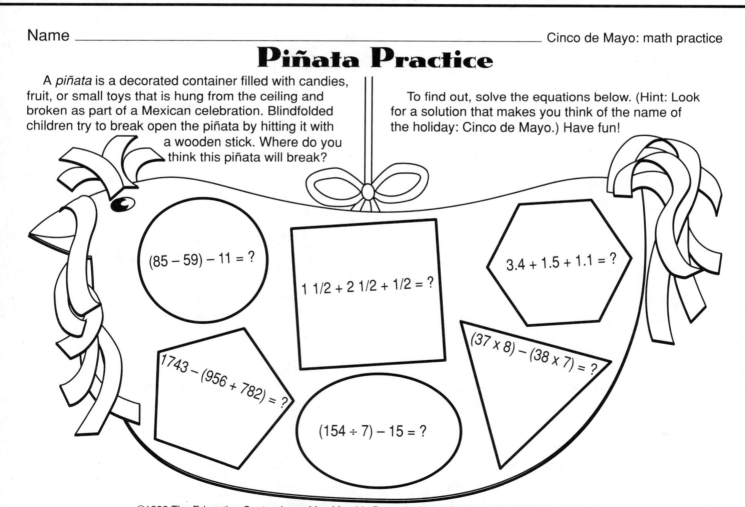

$(85 - 59) - 11 = ?$

$1\ 1/2 + 2\ 1/2 + 1/2 = ?$

$3.4 + 1.5 + 1.1 = ?$

$1743 - (956 + 782) = ?$

$(37 \times 8) - (38 \times 7) = ?$

$(154 \div 7) - 15 = ?$

Note To The Teacher: Provide each student with a black crayon. Remind students to complete the operations in parentheses first.

Be Kind To ANIMALS WEEK ®

In 1915 the American Humane Association founded the country's first national week for animals—Be Kind To Animals Week®. Since that time, this special observance, which promotes humane care and kindness toward animals, has been held annually during the first week of May.

Listen To A Local Animal Friend

In observance of Be Kind To Animals Week®, invite a local representative of the S.P.C.A. (Society For The Prevention Of Cruelty To Animals) or a representative from the animal shelter to share the importance of kindness to animals with your class. After the visit, divide the class into small groups. Provide each group with one sheet of poster board and markers. Instruct each group to create an eye-catching poster depicting an act of kindness toward an animal.

Can It!

Encourage your students to help prevent animal hunger by participating in the following activity. Have your class sponsor a schoolwide canned pet-food drive during Be Kind To Animals Week®. Donate the proceeds of the food drive to your local humane society. Your students will feel "meow-velous" about helping the animals in their community!

Animal Activists

Divide your class into groups of four to six students. Challenge each group to prepare a short talk on the importance of being kind to animals. Assign each group a different animal. Direct the group to research its animal, then write an outline on ways to be kind to that animal. Encourage the group to use props and visuals—such as costumes, posters, or dance—to enhance its presentation. Have each group present its talk to the class. Then have the groups visit other classrooms to share their views on humane treatment of animals. After each group has visited another class, ask group members to share their insights and thoughts on the activity.

Actors For Animals

Lights! Cameras! ANIMALS! Use your acting ability to show classmates the importance of being kind to animals. Follow the steps below to create a skit about treating animals kindly. Then perform your skit for the rest of the class.

STEP 1

Brainstorm with your group at least three different ideas for scenes where people are not being kind to animals. List the three ideas on a separate sheet of paper. Next to each idea, note a way the scene could have a happy ending with the animal being treated properly.

STEP 2

Meet with your teacher to decide which idea is best for your group to act out for the class. Circle the idea that your group will act out.

STEP 3

Plan how your group will perform the skit. Use the following questions as guidelines: What is the title of your skit? What will the audience learn about being kind to animals? What parts are needed? Who will play each part? How many scenes are needed? Are costumes and props needed? What will each actor say?

STEP 4

Organize your skit. Are the following ready?
____ costumes
____ props
____ lines for actors

STEP 5

Practice your skit. Does your skit make sense? Does your skit teach the audience about being kind to animals? Does everyone in the group have speaking lines? Do you need more props to make the skit more interesting? Meet with your teacher to set up a performance time and date.

STEP 6

Present your act to the class.

Bonus Box: Pretend you are the theater critic for the local newspaper. Write an honest review of your skit for the newspaper.

©1998 The Education Center, Inc. • *May Monthly Reproducibles* • Grades 4–5 • TEC954

Note To The Teacher: Duplicate one copy of this page for each group of students. Divide the class into groups of three to five students. Meet with each group to help it select an appropriate idea to act out for the class. Give each group time to plan, prepare, and present its skit to the class.

What A Character!

There are many interesting stories with animals as characters! Share your favorites with class-mates, and learn about other new and interesting animal stories by completing the following activities.

A. Fill in the spaces on the left-hand side of the book below. Then share these books with your classmates during a book-sharing session. On the right, fill in the titles that you would like to read after hearing about them in the book-sharing session. Visit the library to find new animal titles that interest you.

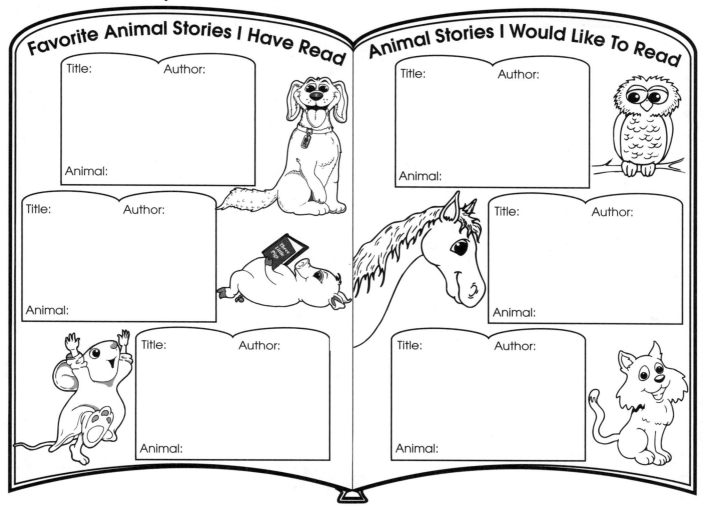

B. Choose a story from the right-hand side of the book above. Read the book. Then, using a 9" x 12" sheet of white paper, create a jacket for the book. Design the cover with an illustration, the title of the book, and the author's name. On the inside of the jacket, answer the following questions:
- What was the main idea of the story?
- What did you learn about animals from this story?
- What was your favorite part of the story?
- What is your opinion of the book? Explain your answer.

Proudly display your finished book jacket for your classmates to read.

©1998 The Education Center, Inc. • *May Monthly Reproducibles* • Grades 4–5 • TEC954

Note To The Teacher: Duplicate one copy of this page for each student. After the student has completed the left-hand side of the book pattern, gather the class for a book-sharing session. Allow students time to visit the library to find an animal story to read.

25

Name(s) _____

26

Dr. Dolittle's Talk Show

Dr. Dolittle is a very unusual character in a famous children's novel. He can speak and understand the languages of all kinds of animals!

Your group is going to prepare a talk show in which Dr. Dolittle talks to different animals about certain issues. Read the animal-related issues listed on the marquis below. Choose one as your group's topic. Then follow the steps below as a guide in creating an original talk show.

Talk-Show Topics

- What is a good age to get your first pet?

- A pet store or an animal shelter? From which is it better to get your pet?

- Spaying and neutering your pet—is it really that important?

- Do exotic animals—such as tigers, ferrets, or snakes—make good pets?

- Is it a good idea to give a child a bunny as an Easter gift?

- Who rules your household? You or your pet?

Step 1: Create A Cast
Decide what kinds of animals will be interviewed on the talk show. List them on a separate sheet of paper. Then assign each team member a different character to portray in the talk show. Remember to assign one group member to play the role of the host—Dr. Dolittle.

Step 2: Brainstorm Interview Questions
Based on the topic of your talk show, brainstorm interview questions that Dr. Dolittle will ask his guests. Write them on a separate sheet of paper.

Step 3: Brainstorm Answers
After Dr. Dolittle asks an animal a question, the character will need to respond with an answer. Think about how each animal in your show will respond to the questions asked. Write possible answers on the sheet with the interview questions.

Step 4: Write A Script
Using the information from the first three steps, write a script for your talk show.

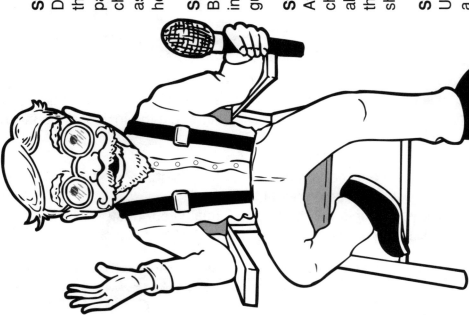

Note To The Teacher: Divide your students into groups of three or four. Give each group one copy of this page to complete as directed.

Mother's Day

In 1907 Anna Jarvis began a campaign for a nationwide observance of Mother's Day. She selected the second Sunday in May for the observance and began the custom of wearing a carnation. It wasn't until May 9, 1914, that Mother's Day received national recognition. On that day President Woodrow Wilson signed a joint resolution of Congress proclaiming Mother's Day as an annual national observance.

A Special Mother

According to legend, the halcyon, a fabled bird, nested at sea around the time of the winter solstice and calmed the waters during this period to protect her young. Point out to students that mothers often go to extraordinary lengths to protect their children. Have your students create cards depicting times when their mothers or guardians protected or nurtured them (for example, by keeping them away from danger or calming them when they were frightened). Then encourage the students to share the legend of the halcyon, and their cards, with their moms or guardians on Mother's Day.

Crazy About Coupons!

Moms will go crazy over clipping these creative coupons from their children! Encourage your students to show their appreciation for their mothers with these easy-to-make coupon books. Make one copy of page 28 for each student. Have each student decorate the cover of the coupon book with an illustration of his mother or appropriate mother figure. Next have him record on each coupon one chore or job he could do to help his mother. Then have the student decorate each coupon and add an expiration date. Direct the student to cut out each coupon and the cover and to staple them together, with the cover on top, along the left edge. Have the student present the coupon book to his mother as a Mother's Day gift.

Special Coupons For A Special Person

Muffins For Mom

Celebrate the special ladies in your students' lives with this tasty idea! Plan a Mother's Day breakfast for the Friday morning prior to Mom's special Sunday. Have each student create an invitation for her mother or appropriate mother figure. Reserve the school cafeteria or another meeting place before the day of the breakfast; then decorate the room with balloons and tissue-paper flowers. Serve a variety of muffins, juice, and coffee. The breakfast takes little preparation and provides a great way to honor mothers!

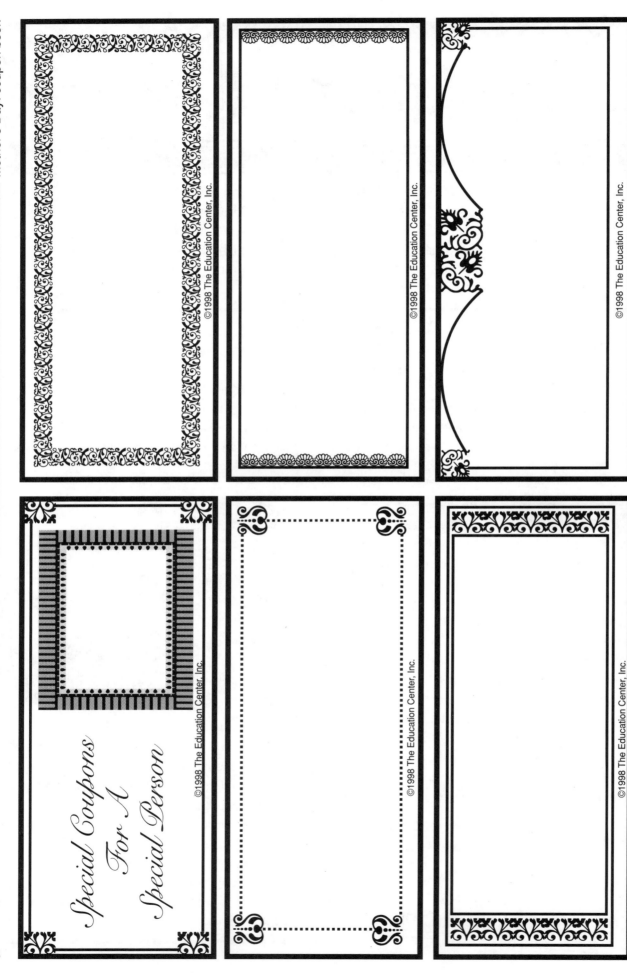

Special Coupons
For A
Special Person

©1998 The Education Center, Inc.

©1998 The Education Center, Inc.

©1998 The Education Center, Inc.

©1998 The Education Center, Inc.

©1998 The Education Center, Inc.

©1998 The Education Center, Inc.

©1998 The Education Center, Inc. • *May Monthly Reproducibles* • Grades 4–5 • TEC954

Note To The Teacher: Use with "Crazy About Coupons!" on page 27.

Words In Need Of Mothering

Each year mothers all over the United States are celebrated on the second Sunday in May. In honor of Mother's Day, here are 20 words that need a little "mothering." That is, each word needs to be completed by using only the letters in the word *mother*. You'll use some of the letters in every word, and you may repeat a letter in some answers. The first one has been done for you.

1. not professional   a m a t e u r
2. to finish something   c __ __ p l __ __ __ __
3. a very dry, sandy area   d __ s __ __ __ __
4. third planet from the sun   __ a __ __ __ __
5. deep ditch dug around a castle   __ __ a __
6. where teeth are   __ __ u __ __
7. a hot cereal   __ a __ __ __ a l
8. to recall or bring back to mind   __ __ __ __ __ b __ __
9. after-school assignment   __ __ __ __ __ w __ __ k
10. games, sports, or hobbies   __ __ c __ __ a __ i __ n
11. half woman, half fish   __ __ __ __ __ a i d
12. a pirate's valuables   __ __ __ __ a s u __ __
13. small, furry rodent   __ a __ s __ __ __ __
14. not rough or bumpy   s __ __ __ __ __ __
15. tool used for hitting nails   __ a __ __ __ __ __
16. a pouchlike body organ   s __ __ __ a c __
17. hard to cut or chew   __ __ u g __
18. degree of heat or cold   __ __ __ __ p __ __ a __ u __ __ __
19. a breakfast food made with eggs and cheese   __ __ __ __ l __ __
20. study of numbers   __ a __ __ __ __ __ a __ i c s

> **Bonus Box:** On the back of this page, list ten words of three or more letters each using the letters in the word *mom*. (Each word should use the letter *m* twice.)

Name _____

❧❧ A Gift For Mom ❧❧

Julia Ward Howe made the first known suggestion for a Mother's Day—a day dedicated to peace—in the United States in 1872.

A department store is having a huge Mother's Day sale! Many items are selling at a discount. Discounts are usually expressed as percents off the regular price.

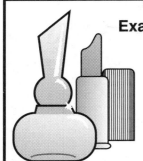

Example: A blouse originally priced at $80 has a discount of 20%.
To find the discount:
Multiply $80 x 20%.
The amount of the *discount* is $16.
To find the sale price:
Subtract the discount from the original price $80 – $16.
The *sale price* is $64.

Directions: The following items are on sale at **30%** off the original price. First find the amount of the discount. Then find the sale price for each item. Use a calculator.

item	original price	discount	sale price
1. dress	$ 85	_____	_____
2. gold watch	$110	_____	_____
3. crystal vase	$ 45	_____	_____
4. perfume	$ 55	_____	_____
5. bubble bath	$ 12	_____	_____
6. blouse	$ 50	_____	_____
7. scarf	$ 22	_____	_____
8. hat	$ 30	_____	_____
9. picture frame	$ 18	_____	_____
10. gourmet chocolates	$ 20	_____	_____

Directions: The following items are on sale at **40%** off the original price. First find the amount of the discount. Then find the sale price for each item. Use a calculator.

11. TV	$225	_____	_____
12. diamond necklace	$350	_____	_____
13. stereo	$200	_____	_____
14. VCR	$175	_____	_____
15. CD player	$ 95	_____	_____

Bonus Box: You can use mental math to find a **10%** discount. Simply move the decimal point of the original price one place to the left. So a 10% discount on the dress is $8.50. A 10% discount on the television is $22.50. Find the 10% discount of the other 13 items above.

Note To The Teacher: Provide each student with a copy of this page and a calculator.

NATIONAL GEOGRAPHY BEE

More than a million students in grades four through eight participated in the First Annual National Geography Bee in May of 1989. The 57 state and territory winners meet at National Geographic Society headquarters in Washington, D.C., for the national competition.

Where Has The Eagle Landed?

Have your students pack their bags for this traveling activity that reviews map skills and geography. Display a large U.S. map on a bulletin board. Duplicate enough copies of the eagle patterns on page 32 for each student to have one. Next provide each student with a strip of paper. Have the student program his strip with a set of clues that pinpoints a specific location in the United States (see example). Direct the student to include one clue that provides the location's latitude and longitude. Fold the strips and place them inside a container near the bulletin board. Each day choose a different strip from the container; then read the clues aloud. Allow students to use maps and reference materials in the classroom to help identify the described location. Have the student who correctly identifies the location tack his eagle pattern onto the appropriate place on the map. (A student cannot answer his own strip of clues.)

Idea contributed by Terry Healy—Manhattan, KS

Salt Lake City, Utah

The eagle is near 40°N and 112°W. He can see mountains, a large city, and a large lake. Where has the eagle landed?

Louisiana

Dear _____ ,

32¢

To: _____

From Sea To Shining Sea

Use the engaging picture book *Stringbean's Trip To The Shining Sea* by Vera B. Williams (Greenwillow Books, 1988) to introduce the following activity on the United States. After reading the book, have the class work together to create a character, similar to Stringbean, who writes to classmates about his journey across America. Using sturdy paper, duplicate one copy of the postcard patterns on page 33 for each student. Next have each student create a picture postcard for a state of his choice. To complete the postcard front, have the student draw and color a scenic attraction that represents the state. Then have him write the name of his state in the banner in the bottom, right-hand corner. To complete the postcard back, have the student write a short note highlighting special facts about the state he has researched. Direct him to address the postcard, complete the postmark, and draw and color a stamp with appropriate postage. Have students assemble their postcards by gluing matching fronts and backs together; then bind the finished postcards into a class book.

Patterns

Use with "Where Has The Eagle Landed?" on page 31.

Patterns

Use with "From Sea To Shining Sea" on page 31.

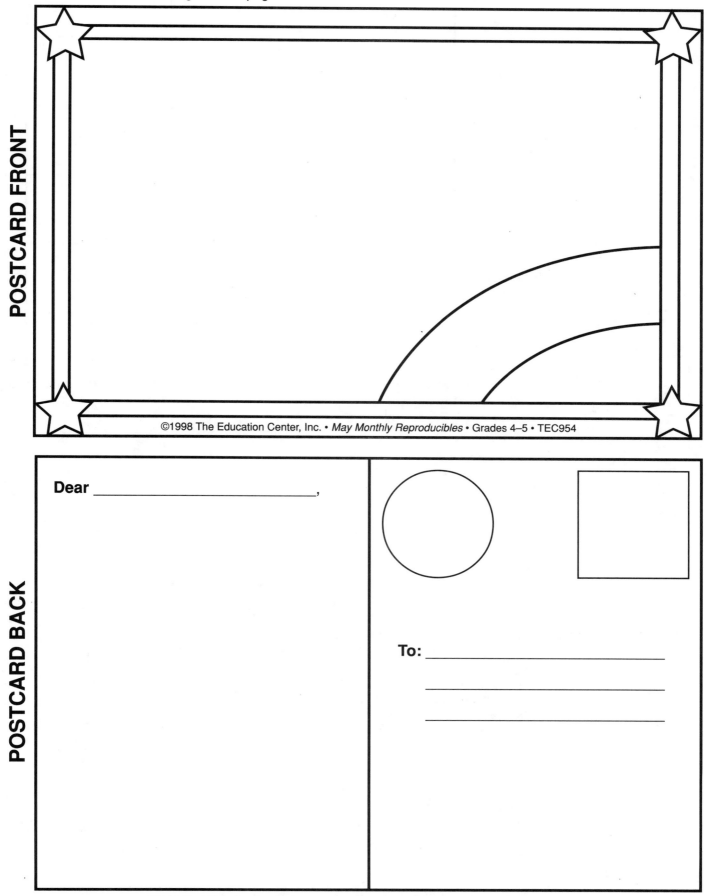

POSTCARD FRONT

©1998 The Education Center, Inc. • *May Monthly Reproducibles* • Grades 4–5 • TEC954

POSTCARD BACK

Dear _____,

To: _____

_____

_____

A "Bee-fuddled" Bee!

Geography Bee Or Bust!

ATLAS

The contest coordinator for the National Geography Bee is incredibly confused! He has lost the list of the contestants' names and their home states. Follow the directions below to help him clear up this contestant confusion!

	North Carolina	New Hampshire	Mississippi	Michigan	Washington	New Mexico
Bernard						
Benjamin						
Bradley						
Bertha						
Betty						
Beatrice						

Directions: Read each clue below. Match each contestant with his or her correct state by placing a ✓ in the grid. Mark an X to show each state that is not a contestant's home.

Clues:

1. All of the boys are from the three westernmost states.

2. Benjamin is from a state in the Northwest.

3. Bernard does not live east of the Mississippi River.

4. Bertha can visit her state's Great Lakes in the summertime.

5. Betty is from a state that borders Canada.

A Tour Around Our Nation's Capital

Bee-atrice Beasley, the bee participant from Bisbee, Arizona, has never visited our nation's capital. While in town for the National Geography Bee, she plans to take a walking tour to see some sites of the capital city. Your job is to help her determine the walking distance to the various locations on the map. Study the map; then draw the scale onto the edge of a sheet of notebook paper. Use this to measure the distances asked for in each of the questions below. Write your answers on the lines provided.

1. About how many kilometers is it from the White House to the Vice President's Residence? _____

2. About how many miles will Bee-atrice have to walk to get to the Lincoln Memorial from the White House? _____

3. If Bee-atrice walks from the Jefferson Memorial to the Lincoln Memorial, then to Georgetown University, about how many miles will she walk? _____

4. If she starts at the White House, is it shorter to walk to the Lincoln Memorial or to the Washington Monument? _____

5. How many miles is the walk from the U.S. Capitol to Georgetown University? _____

6. If Bee-atrice begins walking at the Jefferson Memorial and walks to the National Arboretum, in which direction will she be walking? _____

7. About how many miles will she have to walk to get to the National Zoological Park from the Washington Monument? _____

8. If Bee-atrice walks southwest from the Zoological Park, what is the first point of interest on the map that she will get to? _____

9. Bee-atrice wants to walk from the Lincoln Memorial to the U.S. Capitol, then on to the National Arboretum for an afternoon picnic. About how many kilometers will she walk? _____

10. How many miles is the walk from the White House to Georgetown University? _____

WASHINGTON, DC

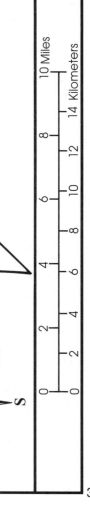

National Zoological Park

Vice President's
Residence

Georgetown
University

White House

U.S. Capitol

Lincoln
Memorial

Washington Monument

Jefferson Memorial

National
Arboretum

Bolling
Air Force
Base

N NE E SE S SW W NW

10 Miles
0 2 4 6 8 10
0 2 4 6 8 10 12 14 Kilometers

Name _____

National Geography Bee: contract

Buzzing Around The United States

Choose a state. Imagine that you are a participant in that state's geography bee. In order to proceed to the national level, you must complete _____ of the activities below. Good luck!

1. Divide a sheet of paper into four sections. Label each section with the name of a different geographical area in your state. Draw and color a scene to illustrate each area.

2. Find a recipe that is native to your state. Copy it onto a card. Prepare it and serve it to your classmates.

3. Fold a large sheet of paper in half. On one side draw a picture of yourself clothed in an outfit you would wear on an average January day in your state. On the other half, draw a similar portrait for an average July day.

4. Design a colorful, scenic travel brochure to encourage tourists to visit your state.

5. Think about the natural resources in your state. Write a letter to the governor of your state expressing your opinions about the conservation of these resources.

6. Write a May weather forecast for a city in your state. Draw a weather map to match your forecast.

7. Make a chart that lists at least four types of geographical landforms, such as lakes, mountains, valleys, and rivers. Then list the names of specific examples of each landform found in your state.

8. Cut out magazine pictures of products made from natural resources found in your state. Glue the pictures onto a large posterboard, cut-out shape of your state. Label the name of each product.

9. Choose a national park that is located in your state. Design two postcards that show scenes from the park.

10. Write an interview with an early settler of your state.

©1998 The Education Center, Inc. • *May Monthly Reproducibles* • Grades 4–5 • TEC954

Note To The Teacher: Before duplicating student copies, program a copy of this contract with the number of activities you want students to complete. The activities on this page can be assigned to individual students, student pairs, or groups.

36

Wright Brothers
Receive First Airplane Patent

Brothers Orville and Wilbur Wright invented and built the world's first airplane. They made their first successful flight in an area near Kitty Hawk, North Carolina, in 1903. They furthered their accomplishments by receiving the first airplane patent on May 22, 1906.

Writing The "Wright" Way

Use the following writing prompts to stimulate your students into doing some high-flying writing this month:

- The Wright brothers studied birds when they were learning about flight. Imagine you are a bird. Describe what it is like to fly.
- Wilbur once stated, "From the time we were little children, my brother Orville and myself lived together, played together, worked together, and, in fact, thought together." Write an essay titled "Working With My Brother/Sister."
- The Wright brothers experienced many failures and disappointments along the road to success. Write a story (real or fiction) about a character who has a dream or goal but has trouble finding success.
- The Wright brothers were inventors. Think about the qualities and skills needed to be a successful inventor. Then write a want ad for an inventor.
- Write a letter to Wilbur and Orville. Include a paragraph in your letter explaining flight today.

May—A Month For Flying

Create an eye-catching display of flight-related events that took place in May with the following idea. Cover a bulletin board with blue paper. Cut a supply of wing patterns from index cards. Write each flight fact from the list below on a different wing cutout. Fold each wing cutout in the middle to create a 3-D effect. Then staple the wings to the bulletin board, adding a sun and clouds for a finishing touch.

Flight Facts

- On May 31, 1919, the first wedding in an airplane took place.
- On May 20, 1927, Charles Lindbergh left New York on the first solo transatlantic flight.
- The first airline stewardesses started work in May of 1930.
- Amelia Earhart began a solo flight across the Atlantic Ocean on May 20, 1932.
- The first cross-country helicopter flight began in Stratford, Connecticut, on May 13, 1942.
- May 26, 1951, is the birthday of the first American woman in space, Sally Ride.
- On May 18, 1953, Jacqueline Cochran became the first woman pilot to fly faster than the speed of sound.
- Alan B. Shepard became the first American in space on May 5, 1961.
- In May of 1976, the Concorde Supersonic Jet began regular four-hour flights between Paris and Washington, DC.
- On May 12, 1980, Maxie Anderson and his son Kris began the first nonstop balloon flight across North America.

The Story Of The Wright Brothers

Pilot your way through the lives of Orville and Wilbur Wright. Read the facts about the Wright brothers in the boxes below. Number each plane so that the story is in the correct order. Next cut out the boxes and make a timeline by gluing them in order on a sheet of paper.

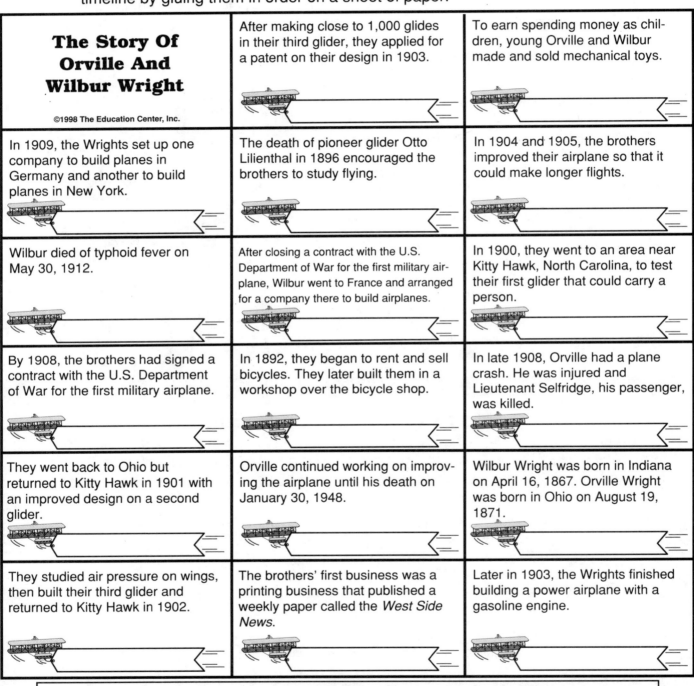

The Story Of Orville And Wilbur Wright ©1998 The Education Center, Inc.	After making close to 1,000 glides in their third glider, they applied for a patent on their design in 1903.	To earn spending money as children, young Orville and Wilbur made and sold mechanical toys.
In 1909, the Wrights set up one company to build planes in Germany and another to build planes in New York.	The death of pioneer glider Otto Lilienthal in 1896 encouraged the brothers to study flying.	In 1904 and 1905, the brothers improved their airplane so that it could make longer flights.
Wilbur died of typhoid fever on May 30, 1912.	After closing a contract with the U.S. Department of War for the first military airplane, Wilbur went to France and arranged for a company there to build airplanes.	In 1900, they went to an area near Kitty Hawk, North Carolina, to test their first glider that could carry a person.
By 1908, the brothers had signed a contract with the U.S. Department of War for the first military airplane.	In 1892, they began to rent and sell bicycles. They later built them in a workshop over the bicycle shop.	In late 1908, Orville had a plane crash. He was injured and Lieutenant Selfridge, his passenger, was killed.
They went back to Ohio but returned to Kitty Hawk in 1901 with an improved design on a second glider.	Orville continued working on improving the airplane until his death on January 30, 1948.	Wilbur Wright was born in Indiana on April 16, 1867. Orville Wright was born in Ohio on August 19, 1871.
They studied air pressure on wings, then built their third glider and returned to Kitty Hawk in 1902.	The brothers' first business was a printing business that published a weekly paper called the *West Side News*.	Later in 1903, the Wrights finished building a power airplane with a gasoline engine.

Bonus Box: Research to find out what the Wright brothers' glider looked like. Draw a picture of it; then display it in your classroom.

Note To The Teacher: Duplicate one copy of this page for each student. Provide the student with scissors, glue, and a 9" x 12" sheet of colored construction paper.

Up, Up, And Away!

You and your partner will have just "plane" fun with the activity below! Follow the directions to learn about designing airplanes.

Materials: 2 sheets of drawing paper, 1 stopwatch or watch, 1 tape measure or yardstick, masking tape, marker

Procedure:
1. Design an airplane and then make it using one sheet of paper. Label it "Airplane 1."
2. Mark a starting point on the ground with a small strip of masking tape.
3. Stand behind the tape and toss Airplane 1.
4. Using a stopwatch (or watch) and tape measure (or yardstick), measure the time and distance the plane travels.
5. Record the results in Chart 1. Then repeat Steps 3–4 two more times and record your results.
6. Discuss with your partner how the airplane design could be improved so that it would fly for a longer distance and for a greater amount of time.
7. Using your ideas for improving the design, make a second airplane.
8. Repeat Steps 3–4 with Airplane 2, recording the results in Chart 2.

Chart 1

Airplane 1	Time In Air	Distance Traveled
Trial 1		
Trial 2		
Trial 3		

Chart 2

Airplane 2	Time In Air	Distance Traveled
Trial 1		
Trial 2		
Trial 3		

Conclusions: Compare the results from both charts. Which design worked best? Explain your

answer. _____

_____

_____

Note To The Teacher: Duplicate one copy of this page for each pair of students. Provide each pair with the items in the materials list. For safety, have pairs fly their airplanes outdoors, in a gym, or in a hallway with little traffic.

NEWSFLASH—Man Can Fly!

When the Wright brothers made their historic flight on December 17, 1903, only a few newspapers told the story. Travel back in time to December of 1903, and pretend that you are a news reporter witnessing the first flight. Use the steps below as a guide for writing a news article about this historic event.

A. Remember that every good reporter finds out the facts first. Answer the questions below. Use the back of this sheet if you need more space.

WHO is the story about? _____

WHAT happened? _____
_____

WHEN did it happen? _____
_____

WHERE did it happen? _____
_____

WHY did it happen? _____
_____
_____

HOW did it happen? _____
_____
_____

B. As a reporter, what other questions would you ask the Wright brothers about this historic event? Write at least three questions on the lines below; then, on the back of this sheet, answer the questions the way you think the brothers would have responded. _____
_____
_____

C. Now it's time to begin writing. Use the information in parts A and B to write your news story on another piece of paper. After you've completed a rough draft, have a classmate edit your news story. Make corrections and then rewrite your story in final form.

D. Draw an illustration to go with your news story. Add a caption.

Note To The Teacher: Duplicate one copy of this page for each student. Supply the class with a variety of resource materials on the Wright brothers.

Wright Brothers Receive First Airplane Patent: creative thinking

Patent Pending

A *patent* is a special document issued by the U.S. Patent and Trademark Office. It gives an inventor legal rights to his idea and invention. Since it takes about a year to get a patent approved, an inventor can begin making and selling his invention with a special seal on it that says "Patent Pending."

A. Imagine that you are an inventor. Try to think of a new invention for each of the categories listed below in the Inventor's Log Book. Write your ideas in the appropriate spaces. Remember, to be eligible for a patent, your invention must be new, useful, and original (never made before).

B. Select one of your ideas to develop into an invention. Draw a picture of your completed invention in the space below. Then write a detailed description of it on the lines provided.

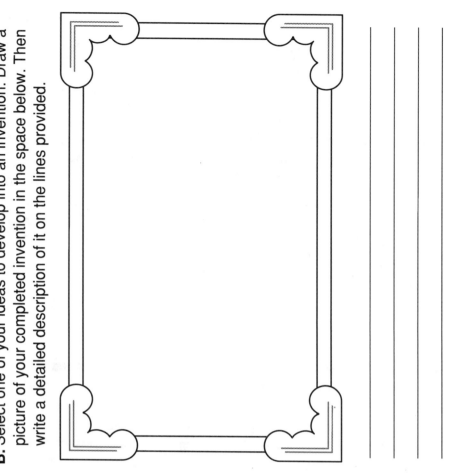

Inventor's Log Book

Form Of Transportation: _____

Food: _____

Type Of Clothing: _____

Game: _____

Tool: _____

Other: _____

_____
_____
_____
_____

Note To The Teacher: Duplicate one copy of this page for each student. After each student has completed his sheet, have him present his invention to the class. After his presentation, reward the student with a homemade patent sticker.

Just "Plane" Math

Practice your basic operational skills with the high-flying problems below. Solve each problem; then write each answer in the space provided.

1. Wilbur was born on April 16. Orville was born on August 19. How many days are there between their birthdays?

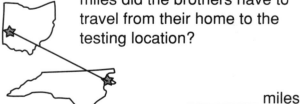

_____ days

4. The Wrights' first glider measured 16 feet from wing tip to wing tip. Their first power airplane had wings that were 40 1/2 feet long. How much bigger was the power airplane than the glider?

_____ feet

2. Wilbur was born in 1867, and Orville was born in 1871. They started a bicycle business when they were 25 and 21 years old. In what year did they start the bicycle business?

_____

5. On December 17, 1903, the Wrights made their historic first flight. Orville flew a distance of 120 feet for 12 seconds. Wilbur flew 852 feet for 59 seconds. To the nearest second, about how fast was each man traveling?

Orville = _____ feet per second

Wilbur = _____ feet per second

3. The Wright brothers lived in Dayton, Ohio, but selected an area near Kitty Hawk, North Carolina, as the testing location for their first glider. On a map with a scale of 1 inch = 200 miles, Dayton is about 2 1/2 inches away from Kitty Hawk. How many miles did the brothers have to travel from their home to the testing location?

_____ miles

6. One of the Wright brothers' students, Calbraith Rodgers, completed the first American coast-to-coast flight in 1911. He flew 4,231 miles from Long Island, New York, to Long Beach, California. He was in the air for about 82 hours. Calculate the average mph (miles per hour) he traveled.

_____ mph

NATIONAL SCIENCE WEEK

National Science Week is observed each year during the third week of May.

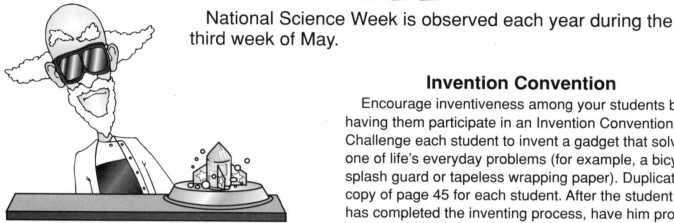

Plop! Plop! Fizz! Fizz!

Bring a little springtime fun into your science lessons with this experiment on rocket propulsion! Divide students into pairs; then give each child one copy of page 44. Provide each student pair with the materials listed. Direct each pair to follow the steps on the sheet as a review of the scientific method. Have student volunteers explain what they think caused the rocket to launch. *(When the tablet was placed in the water, a gas began to form. As the pressure inside the canister increased, it forced the lid off the rocket and caused it to shoot upward. When rocket propulsion occurs, gas builds up or expands inside the rocket. This gas presses against the rocket in all directions. The gas pushing on one side of the rocket is balanced by the gas pushing against the opposite side. The gas flowing to the rocket's rear escapes and is not balanced by gas pressure in the front of the rocket. This uneven distribution of gas pressure propels the rocket upward.)*

Extend the activity by introducing Sir Isaac Newton's third law of motion: For every action, there is an equal and opposite reaction. Give each pair of students an aluminum pie plate. Have the pair place its rocket on the inverted plate. After liftoff, have students observe the indention left in the aluminum plate and compare it to the third law of motion.

Invention Convention

Encourage inventiveness among your students by having them participate in an Invention Convention. Challenge each student to invent a gadget that solves one of life's everyday problems (for example, a bicycle splash guard or tapeless wrapping paper). Duplicate a copy of page 45 for each student. After the student has completed the inventing process, have him provide the necessary patent information on the sheet. Direct the student to turn in a working model of his invention with the patent application. Following the submission of all applications, hold a class discussion and evaluation of the entries. Award patent certificates to all students whose inventions work.

Science Stumpers

Are your students stumped by certain science questions? Even the world's top scientists still grapple with questions such as these:
- Why do newborn babies smile?
- Why do we grow old?
- Why does crying make us feel better?
- Why do pods of whales beach themselves?

Ask each student to write down one science question that she would like explained. Collect all questions and write them on a large piece of chart paper to be displayed. Create teams of two or three students. Direct each team to select one question that it would like to research. After a trip to the library, invite each group to share its findings.

Name _____

Plop! Plop! Fizz! Fizz!

Have a BLAST reviewing the steps of the scientific method with the following activity on rockets!

Problem: How can a film canister and an antacid tablet work like a rocket?

Materials:
1 Fuji® film canister with a lid, 1 Alka-Seltzer® tablet, water, tape, scissors

Procedure:
1. Cut along the solid lines on each of the four fins below. Fold the flaps on each fin along the dashed lines in opposite directions. Then tape each fin to the film canister (lid side down) as shown in Figure 1. Do <u>not</u> tape the fins to the lid.
2. Cut out the nose cone. Shape the semi-circle into a cone and secure it with tape. Using tape, attach the cone to the top of the film canister (opposite end of lid) as shown in Figure 2.
3. Remove the lid of the canister. Fill the canister one-third full of water. Place the Alka-Seltzer® tablet in the canister.
4. Very quickly snap the canister lid in place. Turn the rocket right side up, place it on a flat surface, and stand back for liftoff!
5. Record the results and your conclusion below.

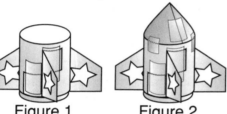

Figure 1   Figure 2

Results: _____
_____
_____
_____
_____
_____
_____

Conclusion: _____
_____
_____
_____

Patterns

Nose Cone

Fins

Note To The Teacher: Use with "Plop! Plop! Fizz! Fizz!" on page 43. Provide each pair of students with the materials listed above. It is important that a Fuji® film canister and lid be used. The lid's design is important to the success of the rocket's blastoff.

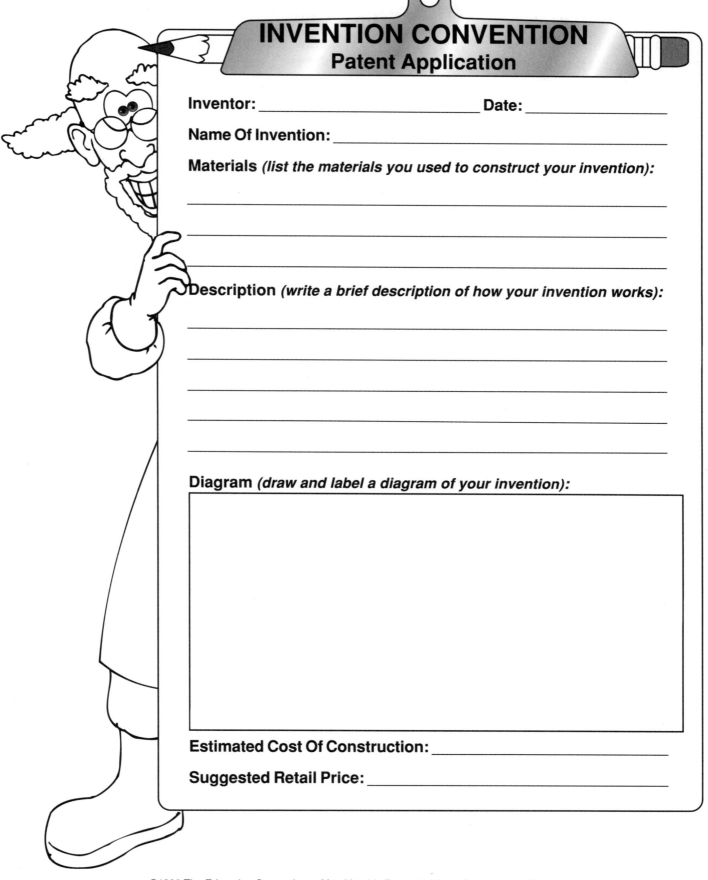

INVENTION CONVENTION
Patent Application

Inventor: _____ Date: _____

Name Of Invention: _____

Materials *(list the materials you used to construct your invention):*

_____

_____

_____

Description *(write a brief description of how your invention works):*

_____

_____

_____

_____

_____

Diagram *(draw and label a diagram of your invention):*

Estimated Cost Of Construction: _____

Suggested Retail Price: _____

Scientists Who Helped Shape Our World

Throughout history, men and women have made meaningful contributions into many areas of science. The list below includes just a few of these notable scientists.

Choose a famous scientist below to research. Find out some information about his or her early life. List some of this person's accomplishments in science. Then follow the instructions for making a shape booklet.

Carl Sagan, astronomer, author, and educator	**Mae Jemison,** astronaut and physician
Dian Fossey, zoologist	**Margaret Mead,** anthropologist
Edwin Land, inventor and scientist	**Mary Leakey,** anthropologist
Eloy Rodriguez, plant chemist and biologist	**Rachel Carson,** marine biologist
J. Robert Oppenheimer, physicist	**Raymond Kurzweil,** inventor
James D. Watson, biologist	**Sally Ride,** astronaut
Jane Goodall, zoologist	**Seymour Cray,** computer designer
John Bardeen, physicist	**Shannon Lucid,** astronaut and biochemist
Linus Pauling, chemist	**Shirley Ann Jackson,** physicist
Louis Leakey, anthropologist	**Stephen Jay Gould,** paleontologist and educator

Step 1

Step 2

Step 3

Materials:
one 9" x 12" sheet of light-colored construction paper
4 sheets of 6" x 9" white drawing paper
markers or colored pencils
scissors
stapler

Steps:

1. Fold the sheet of construction paper in half, greeting-card fashion. Then, starting at the fold of the paper, draw a shape that represents the famous scientist you've researched. (Make sure that the left side of your shape rests on the fold.)

2. Place the sheets of white drawing paper inside the folded construction paper. Make sure that the left edges of the paper meet the fold line.

3. Staple the papers together at the fold. Title, decorate, and color the cover of your booklet.

4. Carefully cut out the shape to form your booklet. Then write your researched information on the inside pages.

Step 4

The ABCs Of Science

So you say you know your ABCs? Team up with a partner and see how well you know your *science* ABCs! Gather together some helpful books, such as your science text and encyclopedias. Try to fill in as many blanks as possible.

A is for _____, a cold-blooded vertebrate that can live in water or on land.

B is for _____. There are a total of six on Earth, each differing from another by its rainfall, temperature, and plant and animal life.

C is for _____, an animal that eats only (or primarily) other animals. An example is a/an _____.

D is for _____, a unit of measure for loudness.

E is for _____. Two types are nuclear and solar.

F is for _____, or any kind of push or pull.

G is for _____, the science that deals with the history of the earth and its life as recorded in rocks.

H is for _____, a powerful storm that forms over the ocean. Its wind speeds may be more than _____ miles per hour.

I is for _____, the largest group of arthropods. Each consists of three body segments, _____ legs, and two antennae.

J is for _____, the largest planet in our solar system. It rotates once every _____ hours and 55 minutes.

K is for _____, the body organ that removes most of the waste water from the blood.

L is for _____, one of the three states of matter that has a definite volume but no definite shape.

M is for _____, one of the groups of elements. Most substances in this group are shiny and are good conductors.

N is for _____, the center of an atom. It is the home for _____ and protons.

O is for _____, the path of Earth around the Sun.

P is for _____, the food-making process in a plant.

Q is for _____, a mineral made of silicon and oxygen.

R is for _____, a cold-blooded animal with scaly skin. Most live on land. An example of this animal is a/an _____.

S is for _____, the dirty haze that forms when air pollution combines with moisture in the air.

T is for _____, the sound accompanying lightning.

U is for _____, a type of sun ray that is harmful to life.

V is for _____, the type of blood vessel that carries deoxygenated blood toward the heart.

W is for _____, the pull of gravity on an object.

X is for _____, the special tubes that carry water and minerals from the roots to the leaves in a plant.

Y is for _____, a recently born or hatched animal.

Z is for _____, a type of African mammal with black and white stripes.

Note To The Teacher: Duplicate one copy of this page for each pair of students. Provide a treat for the team who completes the page first with the most correct answers.

47

Name _____

National Science Week: analogies

Scientific Analogies

An **analogy** compares a likeness between two objects that are otherwise unlike. Read the analogies below. Observe each one carefully and try to find the missing word for each one. The clue is to discover how the words in the first pair go together.

Example: *Dog* is to *puppy* as *cat* is to _____.

A puppy is a baby dog, so what is a baby cat? If you guessed *kitten* you are absolutely correct!

Now use your scientific brainpower to determine the clues that will help you solve each analogy below!

1. *Heart* is to *circulation* as *stomach* is to _____.

2. *Rodent* is to *mammal* as *beetle* is to _____.

3. *C* is to *Celsius* as *F* is to _____.

4. *Incisor* is to *cut* as *molar* is to _____.

5. *Elephant* is to *tusk* as *rattlesnake* is to _____.

6. *Moon* is to *satellite* as *Earth* is to _____.

7. *Lunar* is to *Moon* as *solar* is to _____.

8. *Oxygen* is to *inhale* as *carbon dioxide* is to _____.

9. *Drizzle* is to *downpour* as *flurry* is to _____.

10. *Buffalo* is to *mammal* as *alligator* is to _____.

11. *Lobster* is to *shell* as *trout* is to _____.

12. *Cabbage* is to *leaf* as *carrot* is to _____.

13. *Galaxy* is to *star* as *forest* is to _____.

14. *Butterfly* is to *nectar* as *mosquito* is to _____.

15. *Spider* is to *invertebrate* as *whale* is to _____.

16. *Bee* is to *swarm* as *wolf* is to _____.

17. *Brain* is to *nervous system* as *artery* is to _____.

18. *Wood* is to *solid* as *air* is to _____.

Bonus Box: Think of some more scientific analogies. Write each one on the back of this page, leaving out the last word. Exchange papers with a classmate and complete each other's analogies.

48

©1998 The Education Center, Inc. • *May Monthly Reproducibles* • Grades 4–5 • TEC954 • Key p. 64

Pennies From Mars?

Problem: What makes a penny turn green?

Materials: 1 small saucer, 1 paper towel, vinegar, several pennies

Procedure:
1. Fold the paper towel in half once; then fold it in half again to make a square.
2. Place the towel on the saucer. Pour vinegar into the saucer so that the towel is completely wet.
3. Place the pennies on top of the paper towel.
4. Observe the pennies after 24 hours.

Results: *The tops of the pennies turn green.*

Conclusion: *Vinegar is an acid, which is a chemical. A chemical reaction occurs when this acid combines with the copper penny. A new substance called copper acetate, the green coating on the pennies, is formed.*

Homemade Lightning

Problem: What causes lightning?

Materials: 2 balloons, 1 wool mitten

Procedure:
1. Blow up both balloons.
2. Rub one balloon on the mitten. Rub the other balloon against a wall.
3. Make the room dark. Slowly move the two balloons toward each other. What happens?

Results: *You see light sparks as the balloons get closer together.*

Conclusion: *The balloons, the wall, and the mitten have both negative and positive electrical charges in them. When these objects are rubbed together, the charges change. One balloon becomes more negatively charged, and the other becomes more positively charged. Opposite charges are attracted to each other. When the balloons are moved together, the one that is more positive is attracted to the one that is more negative. The tiny negatively charged particles begin to jump toward the positive balloon. This creates static electricity.*

    Lightning is formed in a similar fashion. The clouds and the ground have opposite charges, so the negative particles in the clouds begin to jump toward the positive particles of the ground. This creates static electricity, which is why lightning is seen.

Note To The Teacher: Duplicate a copy of this page for each student. Place materials in centers so end-of-the-year science activities may be completed during free time. Or send home this page and page 50 to be used for summertime science fun.

We've Got The Beat!

Problem: How can you track changes in your heartbeat?

Materials: one 3-foot-long piece of rubber tubing, 2 plastic funnels, 1 watch with a second hand, masking tape

Procedure:
1. Place the end of one funnel into the end of the tube as shown. Wrap masking tape tightly around the tube to keep the funnel in place. Repeat the process with the second funnel and the other end of the tube.
2. Sit on the couch and relax. Place one funnel over your heart. Put the other funnel over your ear. You should hear your heart beating.
3. Ask someone to time you for 15 seconds. Count the number of heartbeats you hear. Multiply the number of heartbeats by 4. This is your *resting heart rate.*
4. Ask your helper to time you again. Jog in place for one minute. Then use your stethoscope to check your heart rate again. Multiply the number of heartbeats by 4. This is your *active heart rate.*

Results: *When you rest, your heart rate is slower than when you are active.*

Conclusion: *When you exercise, your body burns energy. To burn energy, your cells need more oxygen. Oxygen is brought to your cells through your blood. Your heart pumps the blood so that it moves around your body. When you run, your cells need oxygen right away, so your heart must pump faster.*

And The Race Is On!

Problem: Does sunlight affect the way plants grow?

Materials: 2 same-size shoeboxes with lids, 6 cardboard strips that fit inside the shoeboxes (see illustration), 2 sprouting potatoes, scissors, tape

Procedure:
1. Cut a hole in the end of one shoebox as shown. In each box, tape the cardboard strips so they make a maze. Be sure the lids will fit securely when you are finished.
2. Place one potato in the box with the hole. It should be put at the end of the box opposite the hole. Place the second potato in the other box.
3. Put the lids on both boxes. Place both boxes in a sunny spot, making sure that the hole is facing the light.
4. Once a day for two weeks, check your boxes to see how your potatoes are growing.

Results: *The potato in the box with the hole sprouts a stem that grows around the maze to reach the light. The potato in the other box does not sprout any stems.*

Conclusion: *Plants need light to grow. They will always grow toward the light. This is why the potato in the box with the hole grows around the maze.*

Note To The Teacher: Duplicate a copy of this page for each student. Place materials in centers so end-of-the-year science activities may be completed during free time. Or send home this page and page 49 to be used for summertime science fun.

50

AMERICAN BIKE MONTH

American Bike Month is celebrated during the month of May.

Futuristic Features

The bicycle has come a long way since its invention almost 200 years ago! Share the brief history of bicycles shown below. Then have students identify special features of bikes today. Point out that bicycles will probably continue to change in the future, having new features and improvements. Ask students to imagine what these futuristic bikes might look like. Will they have motors, special equipment, more wheels? Next distribute a sheet of 12" x 18" drawing paper and crayons or colored pencils to each student. Instruct each student to illustrate a bike of the future. Direct the student to name the bicycle, and to label and explain each feature's function. Post the designs in a display titled "Visionary Vehicles."

The first bicycle, invented in 1790, looked like a scooter. It was made of wood and had no pedals. In 1816, it was improved and looked more like today's bicycle. Pedals were not added until 1839. Later, improvements—such as air-filled rubber tires, coaster brakes, and adjustable handlebars—were added.

State-Of-The-Art Road Trip

Roll into a study of your state with this adventurous activity! Divide students into groups of four. Distribute a copy of page 54 and a road map of your state to each group. Remind students how to read a road map using a map key and scale. Then direct each group to imagine it is planning a five-day bike tour of your state. Ask students to describe how they should prepare for such a trip, such as deciding on a route, researching terrain and weather conditions, planning sites to visit and places to stay, packing, and so on. Instruct each group to complete the activity as directed, using its road map for help. Afterward have each group share its planning page. Vary the activity by having each group plan a biking trip using a map of another state.

Spinning Into Bike Safety

The Consumer Product Safety Commission requires that all bicycles sold in the United States meet certain safety standards. Have students describe standards that they think are important, such as having front, rear, and wheel reflectors; properly inflated tires; and brakes and gears that work properly. Point out to students that safety doesn't stop with the proper functioning of a bike, but with its rider. Distribute a copy of page 52 to each student. Have each student complete the activity as directed. Then have students share their responses. Next assign each student a different bike-safety tip. Provide each student with a sheet of 12" x 18" drawing paper and markers or crayons. Direct the student to design a poster promoting the assigned tip. Display completed posters in a school hallway throughout American Bike Month.

Always show the proper signals when slowing, stopping, or turning.

Rules Of The Road

Put your knowledge of bike-safety rules to the test! Listed below are 20 clues about bike safety. Read each clue. Decide if the clue belongs in the *Do* box or the *Don't* box. Then write the clue under the correct heading and cross it off the list.

- Obey all traffic signs on the road.
- Carry passengers on your handlebars.
- Put reflectors on your bike.
- Wear a biking helmet to protect your head from injuries.
- Ride on the road between cars and other vehicles.
- Ride in a single-file line when riding on a road or sidewalk.
- Ignore people and animals that are in your path.
- Show the proper signals when slowing, stopping, or turning.
- Ride on unmarked roads and trails.
- Walk, instead of ride, your bike across busy intersections.
- Take a bike-safety course if one is offered in your area.
- Ride your bike after dark.
- Register your bicycle with the police department.
- Hitch rides on moving cars and other vehicles.
- Race or perform stunts on the road.
- Ride on busy sidewalks.
- Wear brightly colored clothes that can be easily seen.
- Skid through loose gravel, sand, water, or wet leaves.
- Speed up to beat turning vehicles.
- Check your bike regularly to be sure it's in proper working order.

DON'T:

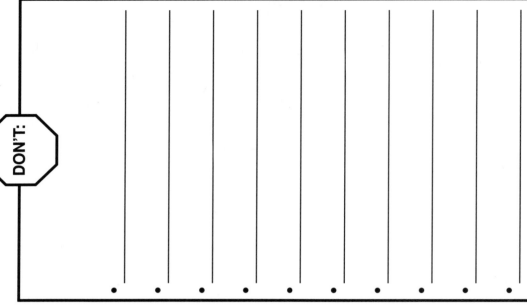

DO:

Obey all traffic signs on the road.

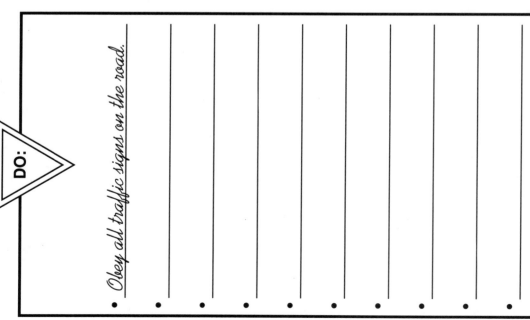

Bonus Box: On another sheet of paper, write a paragraph explaining a time when you needed to use one of the above rules. Be sure to include the when, where, why, and how about the experience.

Note To The Teacher: Use with "Spinning Into Bike Safety" on page 51.

Bike-Trail Trek

The cyclists in the Pedal-Pushin' Club are planning a weekend trip. The club is planning to bike the whole trail around Two-Wheels County. Use the map key and map to answer the questions below. Write your answers in the blanks provided.

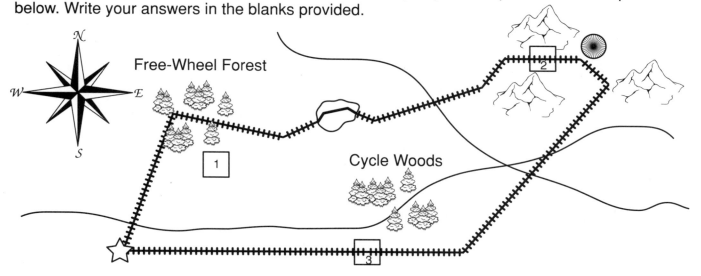

Two-Wheels County

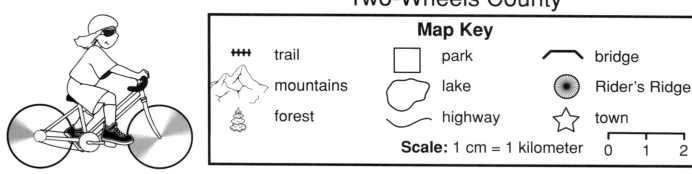

Map Key

┼┼┼ trail	▢ park	⌒ bridge
⛰ mountains	◯ lake	◉ Rider's Ridge
🌲 forest	⌒ highway	☆ town

Scale: 1 cm = 1 kilometer   0   1   2

1. In what county is the trail located? _____

2. In which direction will the cyclists travel if they start in town and ride toward Free-Wheel Forest? _____

3. How many kilometers will the bikers ride through this forest? _____

4. Will the bikers ride on the highway to get to the mountains? _____

5. How many parks will the cyclists travel through? _____

6. What is the distance from the west side of the lake to Rider's Ridge? _____

7. Are the mountains northeast or northwest of Cycle Woods? _____

8. Describe the location of the park through which the trail does *not* pass. _____

9. Is the town closer to Free-Wheel Forest or Park 3? By how many kilometers? _____

10. Find the total distance the cyclists will travel on their trip. _____

Bonus Box: Color each symbol on the map key. Then color the symbols on the map. Be sure the symbols on the map match the symbols on the map key!

Note To The Teacher: Duplicate one copy of this page for each student. If desired, have students complete this page before beginning the activity "State-Of-The-Art Road Trip" described on page 51.

Great State Getaway

Use a road map of your state to help you gear up for one great getaway! Complete the information about your state on the notebook at the left. On the right, draw a map of the biking route you will travel. Include a labeled roadway and the sites you will visit. Be sure to include a key explaining the symbols you create for your map.

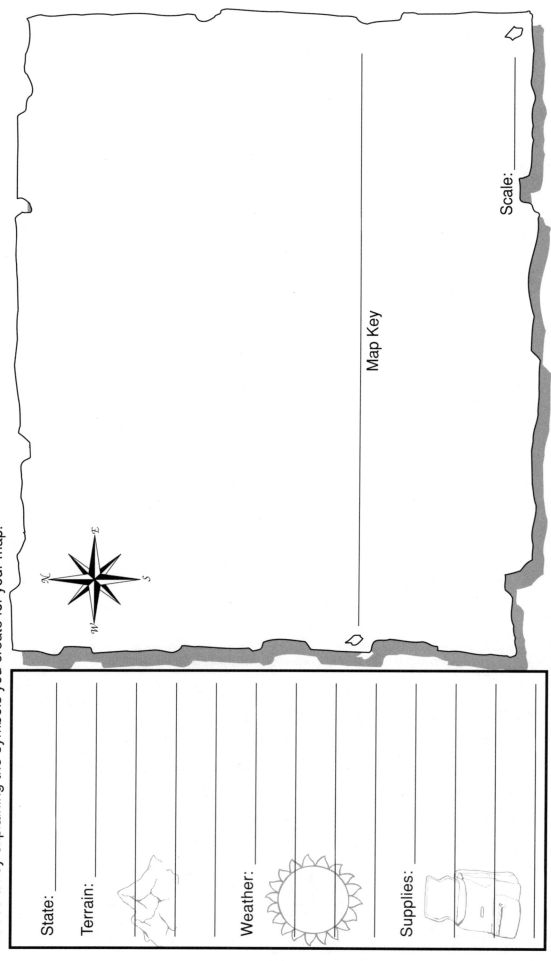

Map Key

Scale: _____

State: _____

Terrain: _____
_____
_____

Weather: _____
_____
_____

Supplies: _____
_____
_____

©1998 The Education Center, Inc. • *May Monthly Reproducibles* • Grades 4–5 • TEC954

Note To The Teacher: Use with "State-Of-The-Art Road Trip" on page 51.

National Spelling Bee Finals

Each year newspapers and other sponsors send about 250 youngsters to Washington, D.C., to participate in the National Spelling Bee Finals. This event is held annually, Wednesday and Thursday of Memorial Day week.

"Washington" capital W... A... S... H...

Class Spelling Bee

In celebration of the National Spelling Bee Finals, hold your own classroom spelling bee with your students. Have each student scour his textbooks, novels, and other reference materials for ten challenging words. Instruct him to write the list of words on a slip of paper, double-checking for correct spelling. Collect your students' lists, put them in a hat or container, and use them in your classroom bee.

exhausted

Draw It! Spell It!

Instead of writing definitions, have your students illustrate their next list of spelling words. Duplicate and distribute one copy of page 56 to each student. Provide each student with crayons, markers, or colored pencils. Select 12 words from your spelling word list for your students to illustrate, or have each student select the 12 words he'd like to illustrate. Your students will find this activity fun and challenging.

Crossword Challenge

Challenge your students to create their own crossword puzzles using their spelling words. Duplicate and distribute two copies of page 57 to each student. Encourage each student to use as many words from the week's spelling list as possible in his puzzle. Instruct the student to number and write a clue for each spelling word used in the puzzle in the appropriate box at the bottom of the reproducible. Tell the student that this will be the key for his puzzle. Next have the student create the blank, numbered puzzle grid on the second copy of page 57. Tell the student to shade in any boxes that are not used in the puzzle. Then have students exchange and solve each other's puzzles.

National Spelling Bee Finals: illustrating spelling words

Draw It! Spell It!

Directions: Select 12 of your spelling words to illustrate. Write each word in a separate blank below. Then draw an illustration above each word that depicts that word's meaning. Be as detailed as possible.

2. _____	3. _____	4. _____
6. _____	7. _____	8. _____
10. _____	11. _____	12. _____
5. _____	9. _____	

©1998 The Education Center, Inc. • *May Monthly Reproducibles* • Grades 4–5 • TEC954

Note To The Teacher: Use with "Draw It! Spell It!" on page 55.

Name _____

Crossword Challenge

Directions: Use as many of your spelling words as possible to create your own crossword puzzle. Write a clue for each word in the appropriate box below.

Across

Down

©1998 The Education Center, Inc. • *May Monthly Reproducibles* • Grades 4–5 • TEC954

Spelling Word Scavenger Hunt

Directions: Examine your spelling word list carefully. See if you can find at least one word for each description below.

Find a word…

1. that has double consonants like the word ba<u>tt</u>le. _____	2. with three or more syllables. _____	3. that has multiple meanings. _____
4. that is new to you. Write its definition here: _____ _____ _____	5. that begins and ends with a vowel. _____	6. that contains double vowels like the word <u>ee</u>l. _____
7. that ends in a vowel. _____	8. that is a plural. _____	9. that begins with a prefix. _____
10. that begins and ends with a consonant. _____	11. that ends with a suffix. _____	12. that can be used as a noun and a verb. _____

MEMORIAL DAY

Memorial Day is an American patriotic holiday that honors those who have died while serving our country in times of war. In 1971 Memorial Day became a national holiday, celebrated on the last Monday in May. People show their respect for the members of the armed services who faithfully served our country in many ways. They decorate grave sites, attend parades, and fly their flags at half-mast until noon.

In The Know

Commemorate Memorial Day by finding out just how much your students know about this holiday. Draw a K-W-L chart on the chalkboard as shown. Ask students to tell you what they already know about Memorial Day. List their responses on the chalkboard under the chart's *K* (Know) section. Next ask students what questions they have about Memorial Day. Do not answer students' questions, just write them under the chart's *W* (Want to know) section. Then have groups of students research to find answers to their questions. (Students can also gather information while completing the reproducible on page 60.) After students complete their research, add their findings to the chart's *L* (Learned) section.

K	W	L
• It has something to do with wars. • Parades are held. • Parents get the day off from work.		

Remembering The Living

Use this occasion to help students remember the service people *currently* serving their country. Give each student a copy of the bordered writing paper on page 62. Have him use the page to write a cheerful letter or poem expressing his appreciation for that service person's help in preserving our freedoms and world peace. Suggest that students color the borders of their papers before you collect them. Take the letters to a local armed services branch office requesting that they be used to add a bit of cheer to a service person's day!

Ranking The Titles

Celebrate Memorial Day with a free-time center activity that helps students learn more about the titles given to military personnel. First make a transparency and a self-checking key of the chart below. Next gather 32 white index cards. Use a red marker to write the following headings on four of the cards: Air Force, Army, Marine Corps, Navy. Use a blue marker to write each title (General, Colonel, etc.) on the remaining cards. Shuffle the cards and band them together; then place the cards and the key in a container. To introduce the center, display the transparency. Explain that the titles are in order of rank. Also point out that different branches of the military have different titles for certain ranks. Then have students use their free time to arrange the container's title cards under their proper headings by rank, then check with the key.

Air Force	Army	Marine Corps	Navy
General	General	General	Admiral
Colonel	Colonel	Colonel	Captain
Major	Major	Major	Lieutenant Commander
Captain	Captain	Captain	Lieutenant
First Lieutenant	First Lieutenant	First Lieutenant	Lieutenant Junior
Staff Sergeant	Sergeant	Sergeant	Petty Officer
Airman	Private	Lance Corporal	Seaman

Memorial Day Flags

Directions: Carefully read each group of words below. If the words make a complete sentence, color the corresponding flag at the bottom of the page. If the words make a run-on sentence, leave the flag blank.

1. Memorial Day is observed on the last Monday in May the holiday began in 1866 to honor and decorate the graves of Civil War soldiers.
2. Now it is a day to honor military personnel who died while serving the United States.
3. Its original name was Decoration Day it was called Decoration Day because military graves are usually decorated with flowers and flags.
4. Memorial Day is celebrated in many different ways.
5. Since the end of World War I, volunteers have sold small red poppies on Memorial Day it is sometimes referred to as Poppy Day.
6. The money from these sales helps disabled veterans.
7. Poppies can be grown in flower gardens.
8. Many organizations take part in parades and special programs on Memorial Day the Boy Scouts and the Girl Scouts like to march in Memorial Day parades.
9. Families visit the graves of all loved ones and bring flowers they also bring wreaths.
10. It is a day when we honor the defenders of our country and remember departed loved ones.

Now rewrite each run-on sentence correctly on the back of this sheet.

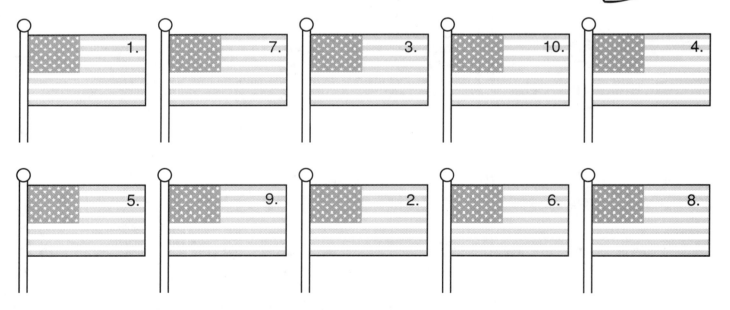

Bonus Box: What is your opinion about women serving in combat? Write your answer on the back of this sheet.

©1998 The Education Center, Inc. • *May Monthly Reproducibles* • Grades 4–5 • TEC954 • Key p. 64

Note To The Teacher: Provide students with red, white, and blue crayons for coloring the flags.

Name _____ Memorial Day: divisibility

Memorial Day Division

Where was the official birthplace of Memorial Day? Follow the directions below to find out!

Directions: Three numbers in each row below have something in common. Circle the letter of the number that does not belong with the other three. Write the circled letters in their corresponding blanks at the bottom of this page. Use the rules for divisibility in the box if you need help.

Rules For Divisibility
Divisible by 2: if last digit is 0, 2, 4, 6, or 8
Divisible by 3: if sum of digits is divisible by 3
Divisible by 5: if last digit is 0 or 5
Divisible by 9: if sum of digits is divisible by 9
Divisible by 10: if last digit is 0

1. Divisible by 9:	18,567(B)	7,543(W)	66,033(S)	99,963(C)
2. Divisible by 2:	648(E)	910(I)	4,389(A)	16,046(U)
3. Divisible by 3:	4,314(D)	690(F)	7,128(J)	8,306(T)
4. Divisible by 5:	20,685(A)	1,010(O)	86,501(E)	22,000(I)
5. Divisible by 10:	890(P)	5,550,510(M)	389,250(N)	8,855,225(R)
6. Divisible by 3:	97,347(S)	36,726(T)	51,399(H)	59,032(L)
7. Divisible by 9:	81,730(O)	7,209(A)	81,540(U)	3,420(E)
8. Divisible by 2:	8,451(O)	78,832(I)	50,304(U)	84,806(E)
9. Divisible by 5:	8,500(H)	707,805(P)	30,114(N)	92,555(M)
10. Divisible by 10:	298,010(I)	47,810(O)	52,220(U)	145,675(E)
11. Divisible by 9:	89,307(G)	1,782(B)	919(W)	20,070(L)
12. Divisible by 2:	248(H)	80,147(Y)	4,776(R)	554(N)
13. Divisible by 3:	6,510(U)	73,911(A)	8,820(E)	299(O)
14. Divisible by 5:	7,560(M)	88,185(C)	3,118(R)	5,000(T)
15. Divisible by 10:	8,650(J)	405(K)	2,590(L)	600,000(N)

The official birthplace of Memorial Day was

___ ___ ___ ___ ___ ___ ___ ___ , ___ ___ ___   ___ ___ ___ ___
1   2   3   4   5   6   7   8   9 10 11   12 13 14 15

Bonus Box: On the back of this sheet, write at least one other number for each of the following: divisible by 2, divisible by 3, divisible by 5, divisible by 9, and divisible by 10.

©1998 The Education Center, Inc. • *May Monthly Reproducibles* • Grades 4–5 • TEC954 • Key p. 64   61

In Appreciation...

Note To The Teacher: Use with "Remembering The Living" on page 59. Give each student crayons for coloring the border of this page after she has completed her writing.

Answer Keys

Page 13

Accept reasonable responses.

1. 13 bicycles; 12 tricycles

2. 16 blocks home; 32 blocks in all

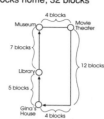

3.

4. Beginning with 1, the even numbers are added in succession (1 + 2, 3 + 4, 7 + 6, 13 + 8, 21 + 10, 31 + 12, 43 + 14…). The next three numbers are 31, 43, and 57.

5. 36

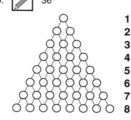

```
              1
             2
            3
           4
          5
         6
        7
       8
```

6. 13 and 7

7. Sean: 58 seconds; Sam: 72 seconds

	60	58	65	72
Sally	✗	✗	✓	✗
Sam	✗	✗	✗	✓
Sue	✓	✗	✗	✗
Sean	✗	✓	✗	✗

8. AB, AC, AD, BC, BD, CD

Page 18

Suggested answers (other answers are possible):
1. triple burger, medium fries, brownie, Macho Meal, large fries
2. triple burger, large fries, medium beverage, cookie
3. small fries, medium beverage
4. cookie, medium beverage
5. two small beverages, one large beverage, double burger, large fries
6. triple burger, medium fries, medium drink, brownie, Munchkin Meal, large drink

Page 20

	Mexico City (bullfight)	Monterrey (national park)	Yucatán Peninsula	Lake Chapala
Carlos	No	Yes	No	No
Luis	Yes	No	No	No
Maria	No	No	No	Yes
Rosita	No	No	Yes	No

Carlos visited Monterrey.
Luis visited Mexico City.
Maria visited Lake Chapala.
Rosita visited the Yucatán Peninsula.

	Video Camera	Postcards	Backpack	Tape Recorder
Carlos	Yes	No	No	No
Luis	No	No	Yes	No
Maria	No	No	No	Yes
Rosita	No	Yes	No	No

Carlos took a video camera.
Luis took a backpack.
Maria took a tape recorder.
Rosita took postcards.

Page 22

(85 − 59) − 11 = 15
1 1/2 + 2 1/2 + 1/2 = 4 1/2
3.4 + 1.5 + 1.1 = 6.0
1743 − (956 + 782) = 5
(154 ÷ 7) − 15 = 7
(37 x 8) − (38 x 7) = 30

The piñata will break open at the pentagon shape. *Cinco* means 5 in Spanish. The pentagon shape has five sides, and the solution to its equation is 5.

Page 29

1. amateur
2. complete
3. desert
4. earth
5. moat
6. mouth
7. oatmeal
8. remember
9. homework
10. recreation
11. mermaid
12. treasure
13. hamster
14. smooth
15. hammer
16. stomach
17. tough
18. temperature
19. omelet
20. mathematics

Page 30

	discount	sale price		discount	sale price
1.	$25.50	$59.50	11.	$90.00	$135.00
2.	$33.00	$77.00	12.	$140.00	$210.00
3.	$13.50	$31.50	13.	$80.00	$120.00
4.	$16.50	$38.50	14.	$70.00	$105.00
5.	$3.60	$8.40	15.	$38.00	$57.00
6.	$15.00	$35.00			
7.	$6.60	$15.40			
8.	$9.00	$21.00			
9.	$5.40	$12.60			
10.	$6.00	$14.00			

Bonus Box answers:

2.	$11.00	7.	$2.20	12.	$35.00
3.	$4.50	8.	$3.00	13.	$20.00
4.	$5.50	9.	$1.80	14.	$17.50
5.	$1.20	10.	$2.00	15.	$9.50
6.	$5.00				

Page 34

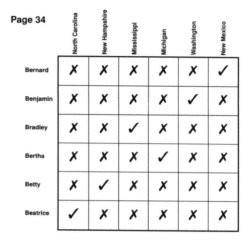

	North Carolina	New Hampshire	Mississippi	Michigan	Washington	New Mexico
Bernard	✗	✗	✗	✗	✗	✓
Benjamin	✗	✗	✗	✗	✓	✗
Bradley	✗	✗	✓	✗	✗	✗
Bertha	✗	✗	✗	✓	✗	✗
Betty	✗	✓	✗	✗	✗	✗
Beatrice	✓	✗	✗	✗	✗	✗

Page 35

1. about 4 kilometers
2. about 1 mile
3. about 3 miles
4. Washington Monument
5. 4 miles
6. NE (northeast)
7. about 3 miles
8. Vice President's Residence
9. about 6.5 kilometers
10. 2 miles

Page 38

1. Wilbur Wright was born in Indiana on April 16, 1867. Orville Wright was born in Ohio on August 19, 1871.
2. To earn spending money as children, young Orville and Wilbur made and sold mechanical toys.
3. The brothers' first business was a printing business that published a weekly paper called the *West Side News*.
4. In 1892, they began to rent and sell bicycles. They later built them in a workshop over the bicycle shop.
5. The death of pioneer glider Otto Lilienthal in 1896 encouraged the brothers to study flying.
6. In 1900, they went to an area near Kitty Hawk, North Carolina, to test their first glider that could carry a person.
7. They went back to Ohio but returned to Kitty Hawk in 1901 with an improved design on a second glider.
8. They studied air pressure on wings, then built their third glider and returned to Kitty Hawk in 1902.
9. After making close to 1,000 glides in their third glider, they applied for a patent on their design in 1903.
10. Later in 1903, the Wrights finished building a power airplane with a gasoline engine.
11. In 1904 and 1905, the brothers improved their airplane so that it could make longer flights.
12. By 1908, the brothers had signed a contract with the U.S. Department of War for the first military airplane.
13. After closing a contract with the U.S. Department of War for the first military airplane, Wilbur went to France and arranged for a company there to build airplanes.
14. In late 1908, Orville had a plane crash. He was injured and Lieutenant Selfridge, his passenger, was killed.
15. In 1909, the Wrights set up one company to build planes in Germany and another to build planes in New York.
16. Wilbur died of typhoid fever on May 30, 1912.
17. Orville continued working on improving the airplane until his death on January 30, 1948.

Answer Keys

Page 42
1. 125 days
2. 1892
3. about 500 miles
4. 24 1/2 feet
5. Orville was traveling about 10 feet per second; Wilbur was traveling about 14 feet per second.
6. about 52 mph

Page 47
A is for **amphibian.**
B is for **biome.**
C is for **carnivore.**/Answers may vary: **lion, tiger, brown bear**
D is for **decibel.**
E is for **energy.**
F is for **force.**
G is for **geology.**
H is for **hurricane.**/72 miles per hour
I is for **insects.**/six legs
J is for **Jupiter.**/9 hours
K is for **kidney.**
L is for **liquid.**
M is for **metal.**
N is for **nucleus.**/neutrons
O is for **orbit.**
P is for **photosynthesis.**
Q is for **quartz.**
R is for **reptile.**/Answers may vary: **alligator, snake, lizard, turtle**
S is for **smog.**
T is for **thunder.**
U is for **ultraviolet.**
V is for **vein.**
W is for **weight.**
X is for **xylem.**
Y is for **young.**
Z is for **zebra.**

Page 48
1. *digestion*
2. *insect*
3. *Fahrenheit*
4. *grind*
5. *fang*
6. *planet*
7. *Sun*
8. *exhale*
9. *blizzard*
10. *reptile*
11. *scales*
12. *root*
13. *tree*
14. *blood*
15. *vertebrate*
16. *pack*
17. *circulatory system*
18. *gas*

Page 52
The order of clues under each heading may vary.

DO:
- Obey all traffic signs on the road.
- Put reflectors on your bike.
- Wear a biking helmet to protect your head from injuries.
- Ride in a single-file line when riding on a road or sidewalk.
- Show the proper signals when slowing, stopping, or turning.
- Walk, instead of ride, your bike across busy intersections.
- Take a bike safety course if one is offered in your area.
- Register your bicycle with the police department.
- Wear brightly colored clothes that can be easily seen.
- Check your bike regularly to be sure it's in proper working order.

DON'T:
- Carry passengers on your handlebars.
- Ride on the road between cars and other vehicles.
- Ignore people and animals that are in your path.
- Ride on unmarked roads and trails.
- Ride your bike after dark.
- Hitch rides on moving cars and other vehicles.
- Race or perform stunts on the road.
- Ride on busy sidewalks.
- Skid through loose gravel, sand, water, or wet leaves.
- Speed up to beat turning vehicles.

Page 53
1. Two-Wheels County
2. northeast
3. 3 kilometers
4. no
5. two
6. about 7 1/2 kilometers
7. northeast
8. Answers will vary. Possible answers include northeast of town, south of Free-Wheel Forest, and southwest of the lake.
9. Free-Wheel Forest; about 2 1/2 kilometers
10. 31 1/2 kilometers

Page 60
1. Memorial Day is observed on the last Monday in May. The holiday began in 1866 to honor and decorate the graves of Civil War soldiers.
3. Its original name was Decoration Day. It was called Decoration Day because military graves are usually decorated with flowers and flags.
5. Since the end of World War I, volunteers have sold small red poppies on Memorial Day. It is sometimes referred to as Poppy Day.
8. Many organizations take part in parades and special programs on Memorial Day. The Boy Scouts and the Girl Scouts like to march in Memorial Day parades.
9. Families visit the graves of all loved ones and bring flowers. They also bring wreaths.

Flags 2, 4, 6, 7, and 10 should be colored.

Page 61
1. 7,543 **W**
2. 4,389 **A**
3. 8,306 **T**
4. 86,501 **E**
5. 8,855,225 **R**
6. 59,032 **L**
7. 81,730 **O**
8. 8,451 **O**
9. 30,114 **N**
10. 145,675 **E**
11. 919 **W**
12. 80,147 **Y**
13. 299 **O**
14. 3,118 **R**
15. 405 **K**

W	A	T	E	R	L	O	O	,	N	E	W		Y	O	R	K
1	2	3	4	5	6	7	8		9	10	11		12	13	14	15

Waterloo, New York, has been recognized by Congress as the official birthplace of Memorial Day. The custom of placing flowers on the graves of war dead began there on May 5, 1866, after the end of the Civil War.